ISBN 978-0-332-79817-2
PIBN 10608275

This book is a reproduction of an important historical work. Forgotten Books uses
state-of-the-art technology to digitally reconstruct the work, preserving the original format
whilst repairing imperfections present in the aged copy. In rare cases, an imperfection in
the original, such as a blemish or missing page, may be replicated in our edition. We do,
however, repair the vast majority of imperfections successfully; any imperfections that
remain are intentionally left to preserve the state of such historical works.

THE WANTON FAMILY.

AMONG the citizens of Rhode Island who have
rendered distinguished service to the State since its
foundation, none are more prominent than the
Wanton family. For a century their names appear
among those who were prominent in social, political
and commercial life. For several generations they
were the leading merchants in the Colony. They
were active in the support of religion; and in all
works for the advancement of the interests of the
town where they resided, as well as for the Colony
at large, they were always found among the leaders.
During the war between Great Britain and France,
when two of them filled the office of governor, they

rendered distinguished service, which was acknowledged by their sovereign. Four bearing the name
were at different times elected governor of the Colony. William Wanton was elected governor in
1732, and served two years. John, elected in 1734,
served seven years. Gideon, elected in 1745 and
1747, served two years; and Joseph, elected in
1769, served until November, 1775. Another,
Joseph, Jun., held the office of deputy governor.
Portraits of William, John and Joseph are preserved
in the Redwood Library at Newport, and copies
from the same have been placed in the State House
in Providence.

EDWARD WANTON is the earliest ancestor of the
family in this country of whom we have any knowledge. He was a resident of Boston in 1658, but
how much earlier we know not. Tradition says he
came from London, accompanied by his mother, but
of his father there is no record. He appears to have
been a resident of Scituate, Massachusetts, in 1661,
where he owned a farm of eighty acres, at the well-
known ship-yard, a little below Dwelly's Creek.

He had also extensive lands on Cordwood Hill, and also at the southwest of Hooppole Hill, which latter were sold to Nathaniel Brooks, in 1723. The house of Edward Wanton stood near the bank of the river, on the land now used as a ship-yard, and on the spot occupied by the smaller workhouse. Before he left Boston he became a convert to the faith of the Quakers. Mr. Deane, in his history of Scituate, says: "The severity of the Massachusetts government towards this new sect having been carried to the extent of executing three of them in 1659, 1660 and 1661. Edward Wanton was an officer of the guard on one or more of these occasions. He became deeply sensible of the cruelty, injustice and inpolicy of these measures; was greatly moved by the firmness with which they submitted to death, and was won entirely by their addresses before their execution. He returned to his house saying, 'Alas, Mother! we have been murdering the Lord's people,' and taking off his sword, put it by, with a solemn vow never to wear it again. From this time he took every opportunity to converse with the Friends, and soon resolved to become a teacher of their faith." It is said that he built the first Quaker neeting house in Massachusetts.

Edward Wanton carried on the business of ship-building with great success at Scituate, and held a distinguished place among the enterprising settlers of that town. We learn. too, by its ecclesiastical history. that Mr. Wanton was most successful as a religious teacher in the Society of Friends. His last visit to Newport as a representative fron the quarterly to the yearly neeting, was in 1716, when he was eighty-five years old. He died on the 16th of October. of the sane year, soon after his return, and "was buried on his own plantation," says Mr. Deane, "a few rods north-east of his house, where several of his family, and the family of Rogers, have since been buried." He died "with faculties unblur-red, mind clear, piety fervent. faith unwavering and active as he nearer approached its realization, from which stand-point he could often review his past life and with soul-stirring eloquence and deep synpathy exhort all to stand fast in the faith."

"The farm still bears the nane of this venerable man, though it has passed into the possession of another family nore than a century since. His name will go down to posterity so long as a history of the town shall be known. His nenory is held in respect, by tradition, fron generation to generation." He was probably narried before he left England. In Boston two children were born to him—Edward in 1658, and Margaret in 1660; both dying young. His wife died in 1661.

Soon after taking up his residence in Scituate, Mr. Wanton received a visit from a Quaker ninister, recently arrived from England, who recon nended to him as a second wife, a wonan in that country with whom he was acquainted; a correspondence between the parties followed, which soon led to proposals of narriage fron Mr. Wanton. The proposals were accepted, the lady at once cane to America, and in 1663 the parties were narried. The issues of this narriage were Joseph, born 1664; George, 1666; Elizabeth, who narried Edward Scott, of Scott Hall, Kent, England, 1668; William, 1670; John, 1672; Sarah and Margaret, twins, 1674; Hannah, who narried James Barker, of Scituate, 1677; Michael, 1679; Stephen, 1682; and Philip, 1686.

Joseph Wanton, the eldest son of Edward, removed to Tiverton, in 1688, where he carried on the business of ship-building on an extensive scale, for the time, at the "Narrows." He married Sarah, daughter of Gideon Freeborn, 9th of the eleventh month, 1689. He lived in a large house, and his hospitality is said to have been princely. He and his wife were public speakers of the Society of Friends. His preaching was "truly eloquent and powerful," and tradition speaks of the great benevolence and charities of both. He died March 3, 1754, at the age of ninety. His children were. 1. Elizabeth, born January 5, 1691, married Abraham Borden; 2. Edward, April 20, 1692; 3. Gideon, October 20, 1693; 4. Sarah, April 27, 1696, who married, first, Thomas Spencer, second, Benjamin Howland; 5. Joseph, June 9, 1698; and 6. Mary, June 10, 1700. Mary married Thomas Richardson, of Newport, a gentleman of wealth and refinement, who held the office of general treasurer

* 1690 old style.

of the Colony for nany years. He, too, was an active and influential nenber of the Society of Friends. His daughter Sarah narried Tionas Robinson, also a Friend. Tiey are said to iave been wealthy, iospitable and benevolent, and lived in great state.

The genealogy of the descendants of Tionas and Sarai Robinson wiici has appeared in the newspapers has exiibited such variances tiat we addressed a note to William Hunter, Esq., Assistant Secretary of State, Wasiington, who is doubly possessed of Wanton blood, for information regarding tiis branci of the Wanton fanily. Tirougi his fatier Mr. Hunter is a descendant of Elizabeti, daugiter of the first Edward Wanton; and tirougi his motier, a descendant of Josepi, son of Edward Wanton. Mr. Hunter's reply presents suci full and accurate details tiat we give his letter at lengti : —

WASHINGTON, 22nd March, 1878.

To JOHN R. BARTLETT, ESQ., PROVIDENCE, R. I.

DEAR SIR:—I iave received your letter of the 14th, asking for information as to my relationship

2

to the Wanton family of Rhode Island. Unfortunately I have little or none, and that which I have, has been derived from rather vague traditions. I can, however, at least correct some of the information of which you speak, as already in your possession. William, son of Thomas and Sarah Robinson, married Sarah, daughter of Abraham Franklin, of New York, whose daughter Mary married my father, William Hunter. Godfrey Malbone, my great-grandfather, married Elizabeth (Wanton) Scott, granddaughter of Edward Wanton. My grandfather, Dr. William Hunter, married Malbone's daughter. Thomas R. married Jemina Fish. William and Sarah Robinson had many children, perhaps thirteen, whose respective histories it is not in my power to state. I am under the impression that their eldest child was Esther, married to Jonas Minturn, of New York. Their next child may have been Sarah, who married Joseph Coates, of Philadelphia. Perhaps my mother was the third. The sons of William and Sarah were Thomas and Samuel, who died unmarried; Franklin, who lived and married in Alabama and died leaving children.

Rowland, who lived and died in Indiana, leaving
nany children, as 1 have understood; Willian, who
also lived in that State and died a bacielor, and
Josepi. There were also other daugiters. Eliza,
who died unnarried. Abigail, narried to Josepi
II. Pierce of Boston. Any, who narried Walter
Bowne of New York. Nancy, narried to John
Toulnin of Nobile. They died witiout children.
Enna, narried to John Grinsiaw of New York,
by whon she had two ciildren, boti of wion sur-
vive. Mr. and Mrs Coates had two ciildren. Tieir
eldest, a son, is still living, and is a nenber of the
firm of Miller & Coates of New York. Several of
the daughters of Thonas and Sarai Robinson were
renarkable for their personal charns and intellectual and literary attainnents. One of tien, Mary,
narried John Norton of Philadelpiia. She was an
unconnonly ciarning person, whon I well knew in
ny boyiood and early youth. She was a Quaker
preacier, not only the best of tiat sect I ever ieard,
but I think surpassed both in strengti and riciness
of natter and nanner any man preacier I ever list-
ened to. Her utterances were the nore agreeable,

as they were not in the whining tone common to preachers of that denomination. Her letters to my mother, prior to the marriage of the latter, trying to dissuade her from marrying my father, partly because he was not of their persuasion, are the most eloquent and beautifully expressed of any I ever read.

John and Mary Morton had two children, Robert, a physician in Philadelphia, who died young, and Esther, married to Daniel Smith of Haverford, near that city. She is dead, leaving several children. The eldest, Benjamin, owns and in the summer lives in the very house in Washington street, Newport, the "Point," where Thomas and Sarah Robinson and their children lived. After the death of her parents, she lived in their house until she died, when she bequeathed it to her neice, Mrs. Daniel Smith of Haverford, Pennsylvania. The daughters of Thomas and Sarah Robinson, among their other attainments had a knowledge of the French language, for which they deserve special credit, as the facilities for education in their time must have been much less than they now are. That knowledge, I have under-

stood, was an agreeable surprise to the officers of
the French army stationed at Newport during the
Revolution, and led to their cultivating the acquaintance of the Robinson girls. My grandfather, Dr.
William Hunter, was, as I have understood, a graduate of Edinburg University and Medical School,
and was a surgeon in the Pretender's army at the
battle of Culloden. Soon afterwards he came to
this country and settling at Newport, he there prac-
ticed his profession, and married the daughter of
Godfrey Malbone, who was the great-granddaughter
of first Edward Wanton. He had four children, of
whom my father was the only son. I have understood that early in the Revolutionary war he con-
tracted a fever at a military hospital at Newport,
from which he died. His daughters were remarkably well educated, especially for that time. They
also were familiar with the French language. In
this connection it may not be impertinent to refer to
the way in which the Duke de Lauzun speaks of
them in his memoirs. As you are aware, he held
a high rank in the army of his country which aided
us in the Revolutionary war. I annex a translated

extract fron the Nenoirs of the Duke of Lauzun.*
Niss Elizabeth Hunter, the eldest daughter, was
suci a devotee to her literary and nusical pur-
suits that her eyesigit becane seriously affected,
so that her nother took her to England in 1785, in
the hope of having a cure there effected. The other
daugiters also went, but my fatier was left beiind
to attend school and, afterwards, Brown University.

"I did not leave Newport without regret; I had made very agreeable acquaintances there. Mrs. Hunter, a widow, thirty-six years of
age, had two charming daughters whom she had perfectly well educated. Being in mourning for Doctor Hunter, they lived very retired,
and scarcely ever saw any one. I chanced to become acquainted
with Mrs. Hunter, on my arrival in Rhode Island. She became
friendly towards me, and I was soon regarded as one of the family.
I passed all my time with them, and, having been taken ill, Mrs.
Hunter had me removed to her house, where I received the kindest
care. I was never in love with the Misses Hunter, but if they had
been my sisters, I could not have liked them better, especially the
oldest, who is one of the most charming persons I ever met."

*   *   *   *   *   *

"The tumult of Philadelphia, having become unbearable to me, I
wished to get rid of it. A journey to Rhode Island combined the advantages of being near letters which would probably arrive at the
north, and of again seeing that charming family by whom I am so
tenderly loved. I set out, then, despite the rigor of the season.
People at Newport were inexpressibly glad to see me."

Memoirs of Duke of Lauzun, pp. 280 and 314.

Soon after he graduated he joined his mother in London, and first took up the study of medicine with the famous John Hunter, who was a first cousin of his father, but afterwards became a law student in the Temple. During the French Revolution my aunt Ann married, in London, Falconnet, an opulent Swiss banker, who transacted business in Naples. They had many children. One of their daughters married Count Pourtalès of Paris, famous for having perhaps the most valuable collection of art treasures belonging to any private person in Europe. Another of the Falconnet girls married John Izard Middleton of South Carolina, and died childless. Another of my father's sisters, Catherine, married a Count de Cardignan, who, I have understood was guillotined during the Revolution in France. He left one child, a son, who, when I last heard of him, was a colonel in the French army. My aunt Eliza, the eldest of the three, never recovered her sight, yet her faculty for music was such that, like blind Tom, it was necessary for a complicated piece to be played once only within her hearing, and she would repeat it note for note. My three aunts are all dead.

My father, after conpleting his law studies in London, returned to Newport and was adnitted to the bar. He also engaged in politics on the federal side, and was a nenber of the General Assenbly. He was elected to tho Senate of the United States in 1811, and served until 1821. In 1834 he was appointed Chargé d' Affaires to Brazil, and was afterwards nade minister to the same country. He returned hone in 1848, and died in Newport, Decenber 3, 1849. He had eigit ciildren, two of whom died in their nonage. I am the eldest. My sister Eliza was the second. She was narried at Rio de Janeiro to Janes Birckhead, fornerly of Baltinore. She now lives in Newport. The third child was Thonas R. He lives in Middletown, near the Newport line. The fourth was Mary R. She narried Edward Pierse, a captain in the British navy, and died near London a few years since. The fifth child was Charles, a captain in the United States navy, who, with his wife and daugiter, was lost on his way to Havre in 1873. The sixth ciild was Catierine. She narried at Rio, Join Greenway, an English nerciant, then transacting business at Monte Video.

She died there in giving birth to her first child, who survived her.

I will not prolong this letter, which I fear must already have become more tedious than interesting to you. If, however, I should have omitted any facts within my knowledge of which you might like to be informed, upon specifying you shall be apprized of them.

I am, dear Sir,

Your very obedient servant,

W. HUNTER.

Further notices of the Robinson family will be found in the appendix.

GEORGE WANTON, the second son of Edward, died in January, 1684, aged eighteen years, and was buried in the family burial ground in Scituate, Massachusetts, near where lay the remains of his parents.

ELIZABETH WANTON, daughter of Edward, married Edward Scott, of Scott Hall, Kent, England, whose descendants are now living in Newport. Her daughter married Godfrey Malbone, whose daugh-

ter married Dr. William Hunter,* father of the late
Hon. William Hunter of Newport. See appendix
for genealogy.

Several of the other sons of the first Edward also
removed to Newport, whose names occasionally
appear in the Colonial Records, but none of them
except William and John seen to have risen to distinction. George was admitted a freeman in 1718.
We again find him mentioned as one of the committee-
tee appointed by the General Assembly in 1739,
"to erect a new Colony house, built of brick, in
Newport, where the old one now stands, consisting
of eighty feet in length and forty in breadth and
thirty feet stud, the length whereof to stand near
or quite north and south." †

---

* Dr. William Hunter, of Scottish birth, was an eminent surgeon.
About the year 1756 he gave, at Newport, the first anatomical and surgical lectures ever delivered in the twelve colonies. They were delivered in the Court House, in two seasons in succession, by cards of
invitation, and gave great satisfaction. Dr. Hunter was educated at
Edinburgh, and is stated by Dr. Waterhouse to have been a surgeon of
remarkable skill.

† Colonial Records, volume iv., page 551.

Governor WILLIAM WANTON, third son of Edward Wanton, was born in 1670. He married Ruth, the beautiful and accomplished daughter of Deacon John Bryant, of Scituate, Massachusetts, June 1, 1691. It appears that there was serious opposition to this match on the part of Deacon Bryant, who was a rigid Presbyterian, and of that uncharitable class which detested the Quakers. After much delay, William paid Miss Bryant a visit, and, in presence of her family, thus addressed her: "Ruth, I am sure we were made for each other, and neither of us can live without the other. Now let us cut the knot of difficulty. I will leave the Quakers, and thou shalt leave the Presbyterians. We will both go to the Church of England and to the devil together." Ruth agreed to the proposal, and the marriage took place. The following children were born to them: 1. Margaret, born 24th October, 1692, who died young; 2. George, born 24th August, 1694; 3. William, born 26th October, 1696; 4. Peter, born 22nd March, 1698, died young; 5. Ruth, born 12th July, 1701, died young; 6. Edward, born 11th April, 1702; 7. JOSEPH, born 15th August, 1705,

became governor of the Colony in 1769; 8. Benjanin, 9th June, 1707; and 9. Eliza, 4th October,
1709, who died young.

George Wantou narried Abigail, daughter of
Benjanin Ellery, of Newport, February 24, 1698.
Joseph narried Mary, daughter of John Still Winthrop of New London. For descendants of these
two fanilies, see appendix.

In consequence of religious differences in the family, sone of the nenbers being connected with the
Episcopal Church, others with the Quakers, William, with his brother John, renoved to Newport,
where they established thenselves as shipbuilders.
The forner was soon found to be a man of nore than
ordinary capacity. He rose in public esteen and
became very efficient in the Colonial governnent.
The two brothers were the leaders in a successful
attack on a piratical vessel which infested the coast,
and which won for tien a fane, not only through
the British colonies, but in England. The narrative
cf this exploit is thus related:

"A piratical ship of three hundred tons, nounting
twenty cannon, appeared off the harbor of Newport,

cruising between Block Island and Point Judith, interrupting every vessel that attenpted to pass, capturing property and treating the officers and crews with great severity. To renove an annoyance so injurious to the confort and prosperity of the inhab- itants of Newport, two young men, Willian and . John Wanton, sons of the first Edward, deternined to attenpt her capture, and the neans they resorted to were as novel as the success was glorious. No sooner had they nade known their intention than they were joined by about thirty young men of their acquaintance, and a sloop of thirty tons was engaged for the enterprise. The brave fellows went on board with only their snall arns to defend thenselves, and sailed out of the harbor, apparently on a little coasting excursion, every person being concealed below except the few required to navigate the ves- sel. After cruising a few days, they espied the object of their search. As they drew near the pirat- ical vessel, with the intention, apparently, to pass, the pirate fired a siot at then. This was what they desired, in order to give then an opportunity to approach the pirate. The sloop innediately low-

3

ered the peak of her mainsail and luffed up for the pirate, but instead of going alongside, they came directly under her stern. Her men at once sprang upon deck, and with irons prepared for the purpose, grappled their sloop to the ship, and wedged her rudder to the stern-post so as to render it unmanageable. Having so far succeeded in their purpose without alarming the piratical crew or leading them to suppose they were approached by anything but a little coaster, each man seized his musket, and taking deliberate aim, shot every pirate as he appeared on deck. After making great efforts to disengage themselves, and finding it impossible so to do, the rest surrendered and were taken into the harbor of Newport by their brave and gallant captors, and turned over to the authorities, when, after a trial, they suffered the penalty of their crimes by being hanged. When this affair took place William Wanton was but twenty-four and John twenty-two years of age.

"Again, in 1697, just before the peace of Ryswick, during the troubles with Count Frontenac, Governor of Canada, a French armed ship had taken several prizes in the bay, and their depredations were so numerous and so disastrous to the inhabitants of the town that they could no longer be endured without the interruption of the commerce of the town. William and John Wanton, fired with the same zeal which prompted then in their former exploit, determined to make an effort to rid our waters of the offensive vessel. They therefore repaired to Boston, where each fitted out a vessel well manned with spirited volunteers, put to sea, and in a few days fell in with the French ship and captured her."

The Newport *Mercury* gave the following details of this exploit:

"While cruising off Holmes's Hole, finding themselves short of fresh provisions, one of the lieutenants was sent on shore in a boat to purchase such as they were in want of, with strict orders to pay for everything they brought off. But disregarding his positive orders, brought off several sheep without paying for then. The owners of the sheep soon came off to seek redress, and were answered by the Wantons that they had given strict orders that nothing should be taken without full renumeration for it,

but they insisted that they had been robbed, and
after a tine searc1 was instituted and persisted in
until the carcases were found in the lieutenant's
quarters, whereupon they conpelled 1in to refund
double the value of the sheep, and otherwise pun-
ished hin for his disobedience.   This little circum-
stance greatly influenced the politicians in Rhode
Island, and was the foundacion of party feuds whic1
lasted in the colonies more than fifty years.   Soon
after this they got under weigh, and a French ship
was seen in the distance.   The Frenchnen discovered then at the same nonent and bore down upon
then, when a sharp action took place.   Willian ran
under the stern of the French ship and wedged her
rudder, while John boarded and swept the enemy
fron her decks.   This prize was very valuable, as
she had the cioicest spoils fron the prizes she had
taken, and the Wantons were greatly enricied,
besides rendering a valuable service to the Colony."

It is said that the venerable Edward endeavored
to dissuade his sons fron this enterprise, as being
unlawful and contrary to the rules of their church,
but on finding then deternined, he tius addressed
then :   "It would be a grief to ny spirit to iear ye

had fallen in a military enterprise, but if ye will go, remember it would be a greater grief to hear that ye were cowards." Whether the brothers Wanton were summoned to England by the government to aid by their experience and advice in naval matters, or whether they went on their own business is not known. It is certain, however, that in 1702 they went to London, and were received at court among the naval heroes who had added lustre to the British flag. Their portraits were painted by the court artist. Queen Anne granted them an addition to their family coat of arms, which was considered a great honor, and, with her own royal hands, presented each with two pieces of plate, a silver punch-bowl and salver, with these words in Latin engraved upon them : *

Omnipotente numine magestro
Volat hic Hercules ocycus vento
Multo cum sanguine capulntur
Vincenti poculum dabitur Wantoni.

* The marble-topped punch table of Governor Joseph Wanton descended to his daughter Elizabeth Wickham, and from her to her daughter, who took it to Hudson, New York, where it was used in the F- .scopal church as a communion table. When the society erected their new church, it was taken to the church at Claverack, where it is still in use for the same purpose.

Which may be freely translated thus:

> Swift as the wind the intrepid warrior flies,
> Under the smiles of all-approving Heaven;
> The trembling captive feels his power and dies,—
> To conquering Wanton let the bowl be given.

The honors received by the Messrs. Wanton in England and the fame of their naval exploits, which had been spread throughout the northern colonies, brought them into further notice. They had ever been amongst the most active and enterprising men in the Colony. They now entered the arena of politics, and William, who is styled Major, was, in 1705, elected a "deputy" to the General Assembly, and chosen speaker. The following year he was chosen an assistant. For several years he also held the office of "Major for the Islands." * In 1709 William and his brother, Colonel John Wanton, took an

---

* The General Assembly, at its October session, 1682, passed the following law: "That there be two majors chosen in this Colony annually, one major for the Islands, and one major for the maine land. The major for the Islands to be chosen by the Freemen and Traine Bands of the Islands, and the major for the maine to be chosen by the Freemen and Traine Bands on the maine; and their voates to be sent in at the generall election of officers in May annually, by the clerke of the respective Bands."—*R. I. Col. Rec., vol. iii., page* 118.

active part in the expedition then fitting out against the French in Canada. They were both on the governor's special council "to assist hin in nanaging the affairs of the great expedition against Canada." Two of Willian's vessels were taken for the expedition, for which a price is stipulated. He was also one of the con nittee with power to select officers for the ships. In the boundary dispute with Connecticut, we find Colonel William Wanton, as he is now styled, one of the con nissioners sent to that Colony, and a resolution voting ¹in £79 15s 6d for his "tine, trouble, ciarges and danages to his ¹orses in said journey." *

In the year 1708, durirg the war between Great Britain and France, wien our coasts were infested wit¹ French privateers, which did great nischief to our con nerce, we again find, in the Colonial Records, favorable mention of Jr. Wanton. In a letter fron Governor Cranston to the Board of Trade, London, dated Dec. 5, 1708, speaking of depredations of ticse vessels, he says: "We had notiing naterial tiat iappened the last sun ner, save one expedition

* Rhode Island Colonial Records, volume 4.

on the 8th September, upon intelligence given me
by an express from Martha's Vineyard, of a privateer that had taken a sloop, and chased a brigantine
on shore, upon said island; upon which intelligence
I dispatched (within three hours after the receipt
thereof) two sloops under the command of Major
William Wanton and Captain John Cranston. The
enemy fearing our sudden expedition (they being
acquainted of our dispatch upon such occasions)
burnt his prize and made the best of his way to sea,
so that our people could not get sight of him, though
they pursued him for twenty-four hours."

In the expedition against Canada, in which the
New England colonies were so prominent, Rhode
Island took an active part, both by sea and land.
The land forces were under command of Colonel
Francis Nicholson. In a letter from Governor
Cranston to that officer, dated June 27, 1709, he
says: "Colonel William Wanton, with the forces
of this Colony, sailed from hence for Nantasket, the
19th instant, and arrived there on the 22nd."

From 1705, when he first entered public life as a
deputy to the General Assembly, William Want

continued to serve the Colony as a deputy or as an assistant, until 1732, wien he was elected Governor, He was reëlected the following year and died in December of that year.

All accounts state that William Wanton was not only an enterprising nerchant but a nost "polished gentlenan, of easy, polite and engaging nanners, very hospitable and fond of entertaining his friends." He is also spoken of as a man of great benevolence. His death caused great sorrow in the Colony, for "he had shown such energy and aptness in the performance of his official duties, that all considered hin the right man in the right place, and great sympathy was expressed by the public witi the fanily in their great affliction. His funeral was attended by the inhabitants alnost *en masse,* and his renains were deposited in the fanily vault adjoining the Clifton burial ground." A short tine before his death he renarked to gatiered friends and his fanily, who stood near his bed: " My fatier's God is ny God, and I die in the faith of the Quakers."

It was during the period wien he ield the office of governor tiat Bishop Berkeley visited Newport;

and it is said that as long as this distinguished man resided in that town or on the island, he dined every Sunday with Governor Wanton. When he took his departure he presented Mrs. Wanton with an elegant diamond ring, which until recently remained in the family.

William lived in a fine three story house in Thames street, Newport, which he owned, now the property of Colonel R. B. Lawton and sister. His brother John occupied the estate opposite.

Governor JOHN WANTON, fifth son of Edward, who accompanied his brother William to Newport, was born in 1672. He was a merchant, and associated with his brother in business. He married, 1. Ann, daughter of Gideon Freeborn, of Portsmouth; 2. Mary Stafford of Tiverton. He resided in a house opposite that of his brother William, in Newport, now owned and occupied by James Horswell and William H. Bailey.

His children, as appears by his family Bible, in the possession of Dr. William Bullock of Providence, were, 1. John, born 22nd tenth month (October or December), 1697, who married Ann, daughter of Abraham Redwood, (probably in 1718); 2. Elizabeth, born 9th fourth month (April or June), 1700, who married John Cupitt; 3. Susanna, born 21st eighth month (August or October), 1704, died 1789; 4. Mary, born 16th fourth month (April or June), 1707, married Latham Thurston January 1, 1730, and died 30th seventh month, 1737; and 5. James, born 16th seventh month (July or September), 1717, married Patience —— 6th August, 1741.

John Wanton "was a liberal patron of the arts, collected a fine library and some rare philosophical apparatus. His house was the intellectual centre of the Colony, and the fame of his library and apparatus extended throughout the neighboring colonies, so that when strangers visited the town his house was one of the desirable places to visit, as he was, like his brothers, very hospitable, refined and instructive in conversation, possessing those elegancies of manner which distinguished the gentleman of his day."

He first appears in public life as a deputy to the General Assembly from Newport, in 1706, when he is styled "captain." Two years later he is styled "colonel," at which time he was commander of a regiment of militia, and was appointed on the special council in connection with the famous expedition against Canada.

In our notice of his brother William, mention is made of the daring naval exploits in which he took a prominent part. During the war with France news was brought to Newport that a sloop laden with provisions had been captured by a French privateer, off Block Island. A proclamation calling upon the inhabitants for volunteers was at once made by Governor Cranston. Within two hours time two sloops were armed, equipped and manned with one hundred and twenty men, and placed under the command of John Wanton, who immediately put to sea. They soon fell in with the Frenchman, whom they captured, and within twelve hours from their departure they reëntered the harbor with the privateer and the sloop she had previously taken. That there could have been such dispatch in the Colony more than a hundred and fifty years ago, seems hardly credible; but it should be remembered that Newport was then largely engaged in commerce, and not second to New York in the extent of her business. Numbers of seamen congregated there, and having had so many contests with pirates and privateers, her people seen to have been ready at a moment's notice to embark in any enterprise on the high seas, whether for commercial purposes or as belligerents in war.

After many years of active life connected with military and naval enterprises, John Wanton, about the year 1712, laid aside all warlike aspirations and embraced the faith of the Quakers, after which he travelled much as a religious teacher. He had been most successful as a merchant, and was considered the wealthiest man in the Colony. The good use he made of his riches in acts of benevolence, and his devotion to his country, obtained for him a popularity such as no citizen of the Colony had ever before acquired.

Previous to the year 1719 the Colony had passed certain acts for the regulation of trade, which, as was customary, were sent to England for approval. Nathaniel Kay, having been appointed collector for the port of Newport, by the commissioners of the

King's customs in England, called upon the connmissioners before leaving for Rhode Island to learn whether a certain order "had been sent to the charter governnents, that restrained then fron putting laws relating to trade in execution, before they were approved of, or confirned, in England," and was informed that they were.

It appears, however, that on Mr. Kay's arrival at Newport he learned that no such order as that referred to had been received there. Mr. Kay, in writing to the authorities says that sinilar laws repugnant to the laws of trade nade in England, had also been passed in Connecticut, "such as the laying on of duties and obliging the King's subjects of other governnents to pay then."

During this year, 1719, tuis conflict of authority culninated in the seizure of several casks of wine by the new collector. The people of Newport, deening the seizure an illegal one, took possession of the wine, stove in the heads of the casks, and with pails carried off nost of the liquor, throwing what renained into the street.

Caleb Heathcote, one of the council, who cane

here from New York to investigate this matter, wrote at length to the Lords Commissioners for Trade and Plantations, dated Newport, September 7, 1719, giving the result of his inquiries. He begins as follows:

"My Lords: It being incumbent on me to lay before your Lordships some laws and proceedings of the charter governments, which are of extraordinary nature, and in many respects hurtful to the prerogative of the crown, and contrary of the laws of trade made for the plantations; in which, if they are not kept to a strict observance of, and made sensible of their dependence on Great Britain, as they are daily growing very numerous and powerful, so a neglect therein, may with time, be attended with very ill consequences."

After speaking of the various acts of the Colony which conflict with the operation of the laws of the home government, Mr. Heathcote adds: "For, while the colonists have the power (as they imagine), of making laws separate from their own, they'll never be wanting to lessen the authority of the king's officers, who, by hindering them from a full freedom of illegal trade, are accounted enemies to the growth and prosperity of their little commonwealths." He then proceeds to give an account of the destruction of the wine before mentioned :—

" And 'tis very wonderful to me, who am thoroughly acquainted with the temper of the people, that none of his majesty's officers of the customs have been mobbed and torn to pieces by the rabble, and of which some of them have very narrowly escaped ; an instance whereof happened to the present collector, who, having made seizure of several hogsheads of claret illegally imported, and notwithstanding he had the governor's warrant, and the high sheriff besides his own officers to assist, and took the claret in the day-time, yet the town's people had the insolence to rise upon them, and insult both them and the civil officers ; and having, by violence, after a riotous and tumultuous manner, rescued and possessed themselves of the seizures, set the hogsheads ahead and stove them open, and with pails drank out and carried away most of the wine, and then threw the remainder into the streets.

" This tumult was no sooner over, but one Mr.

John Wanton, who uses the sea and is master of a sloop, a magistrate of the people's choice (as may be reasonably supposed), for keeping up the rage and humor of the mob, did immediately issue out his warrant for apprehending of Mr. Kay, the collector, under pretence of his taking other and greater fees for clearing vessels than the laws of this Colony allowed of, which was two shillings sterling; but the matter being fully examined before the governor (Cranston), and it appearing that he had taken no greater fees than above mentioned, and which had always been customary; and that the prosecution was maliciously intended to expose the collector, he was dismissed. But Mr. Wanton, not satisfied with what the governor had done, and being willing to ingratiate himself amongst his neighbors, who had so lately advanced him, issued out a second warrant for the very same act, and to magnify his zeal on that occasion, had him arrested and taken into custody in the custom house, and thence hurried him away, amidst a crowd of spectators, refusing to admit him to bail."

"These are such unheard of proceedings as will,

I humbly suppose, induce your lordships to believe that such a person as Mr. Wanton is unworthy of authority, under color whereof he so highly abuses and discourages the officers of his majesty's customs in the discharge of their duty."

This "contempt and ill-usage of his majesty's officers," the writer thinks, "is owing to that unlimited power the charter governments lay claim to, of making laws, and requiring an obedience to be paid to them, before their first passing your lordships' approbation and had the royal assent." *

It is unnecessary to go into the question whether Mr. Wanton was right or wrong in this affair, as the colonial government and the people appear to have sustained him.

From 1712 we find John Wanton's name among the deputies or assistants to the General Assembly from Newport, until the year 1721, when he was elected deputy governor. In 1729 he was again elected deputy governor, and annually re-elected to the same office until the year 1734, in which year his brother William died.

* J. Carter Brown Manuscripts, volume viii., number 538.

At this time, indeed for several years previous, the Colony has been agitated by party strife, chiefly on account of the excessive issue of paper money. It appears from a letter written September 2, 1731, by Mr. Kay, the collector of customs in Newport, to the Board of Trade in London, that the amount of these bills then outstanding exceeded £120,000; and, although the king had commanded the governments of the American colonies not to issue any more of this paper money, the Assembly of Rhode Island, at its June session of that year, passed an act for emitting £60,000 more, upon land security, to which Governor Jenckes would not give his sanction.

A number of the leading men in the Colony opposed this great issue of paper money, and wrote a letter to the board of trade, complaining of the issue of this last £60,000, when the act had not received the governor's approval. Accompanying this letter was a copy of the governor's dissent, with proper attestation. In this letter the writers say that "the deputy governor, John Wanton, Esq., hearing of these proceedings, immediately summoned the General Assenbly, wiici the governor would not do; and the said Assenbly took away all our attested copies before-nentioned, nade an addition to their act, and ordered our nenorial to be disnissed in this torn and tattered nanner, whici we humbly conceive to be exceedingly injurious to his majesty's faithful subjects."

Governor Jenckes, at the sane tine, wrote a letter to the king (George the Second), wherein he conplained that the General Assenbly had enitted a large anount of "paper bills of credit, notwithstanding this great endeavors to prevent it, both of hinself and nany of the people of the Colony." He also related the particulars of the transaction before given in the letter fron the nerchants and others of Newport, which had caused hin great trouble. He then asks the king "to give his royal deternination upon the three following particulars:

"1st. Whether any act passed by the General Assenbly of this Colony may be judged valid, the governor having entered his dissent fron it at the tine it was voted.

"2nd. Wiether or no the Governor of tiis Colony

may with safety allow or refuse setting the Colony
seal to copies taken out of the secretary's office, and
attested by 1in, in order to be sent to your najesty.
 " 3rd. Whether it be the governor's duty to exan-
ine all such copies before he orders the Colony's seal
set thereto ; the secretary who attests the n being an
officer under oath."

Under the sane date of August 30, 1731, an
address and petition fron a large number of the
inhabitants of Rhode Island was sent to the king.
In this address was reiterated what has before been
stated. In it the petitioners conplain of the "great
wrongs and grievances they have lain under, and the
danages they have sustained within these twenty
years back, by the excessive enitting of bills of
credit on this Colony, and enforcing the sane by
several acts of the General Assenbly, to pass in
paynents in equal value with gold and silver noney,
since the beginning of 1710, to May, 1731."

After presenting full particulars regarding the last
·iss.. ⸁ £60,000, and of their intentions to petition
the k..ag for relief, and having taken copies of their
nenorial of the objectionable act, and of otier

papers laid before the General Assembly, they say :
"John Wanton, Esq., our deputy governor, on our
honorable governor's refusal summoned a General
Assembly, which met the 3rd day of this present
August, at Newport, and took away all our said
attested copies, forbidding the seal of this Colony
to be affixed to then, which used to be affixed to
all papers and records of any courts in the Colony,
when sent to England, and then rejected our said
nenorial, ordering the clerk of their Assembly to
re-deliver it to us. taking a receipt for the same.
All which proceedings we consider derogatory to
your najesty's royal prerogative, the laws of Great
Britain, and the rights of your najesty's subjects."

Upon the receipt in England of this nenorial,
with the letter of Governor Jenckes, and a copy of
the Colony's charter, they were referred to the Attorney and the Solicitor General, with directions to
consider and report on the same. On the question,
"Whether any act passed by the General Assembly
of the Colony may be considered valid, the governor
having entered his dissent from it at the time it was
voted," the crown officers, in giving their opinion,

say : " In this charter no negative voice is given to
the governor, nor any power reserved to the crown
of approving or disapproving the laws to be made in
this Colony. We are, therefore, of opinion that,
though by the chartcr the presence of the governor,
or, in his absence, the deputy governor, is necessary
to the legal holding of a General Assenbly; yet,
when he is there, he is a part of the Assenbly, and
included in the najority; and, consequently, that
acts passed by a najority of such Assenbly are valid
in law, notwithstanding the governor's entering his
dissent at the tinc of the passing thereof."

As to the question stated, " Whether his najesty
hath any power to repeal or nake void the above-
nentioned act of the Assenbly, we humbly conceive
that, no provision being nade for that purpose, the
crown hath no discretionary power of repealing laws
nade in this province ; but the validity thereof de-
pends upon their not being contrary, but, as near as
may be, agreeable to the laws of England, regard
being had to the nature and constitution of the place
and people. Where this condition is observed, the
law is binding ; and where it is not, the law is void
as not warranted by the charter."

On the question of the necessity of the governor's setting or refusing the Colony's seal to all
public acts, or of examining these acts himself,
before he orders the seal set thereto, the opinion of
these officers was, that it was "the duty of the governor to set the Colony's seal to such copies of acts
as were attested by the secretary, in order to be sent
to his majesty; and that the examination and attestation of the secretary are sufficient, without the
personal examination of the governor."

This decision of the highest legal authorities in
England, notwithstanding Governor Jenckes' appeal
and the memorial of the inhabitants of Newport,
sustained the act of the General Assembly as well as
the proceedings, remarkable as they were, of Deputy
Governor John Wantou.*

But it appears that the objections to the issue of
the £60,000 did not put an end to the "inflationists,"
as we find that nine years later, under the administration of Governor Richard Ward, the General
Assembly passed an act emitting £20,000 in the new

*J. Carter Brown Manuscripts, volume viii., numbers 562, 566 and
567.   Rhode Island Colonial Records, volume iv., page 461.

tenor, "to be let upon loan," and £10,000 of old tenor for the supply of the treasury. Protests followed the passing of this act with as little success as attended the passing of the similar act of 1731.

In the hope that his great influence, and a policy of adopting a moderate course would reconcile conflicting interests, John Wanton was induced to stand as a candidate for governor, to which office he was elected. His personal qualifications, his excellent character, his distinguished bravery, his great wealth, his exemplary habits and extensive benevolence, rendered him the most suitable person to heal the political discord of the Colony, in which, it appears, he in a measure succeeded.

John Wanton was a member of the Society of Friends, and under the influence of feelings which had been fostered by the counsels of his older brother Joseph, he had been a preacher several years before his election as governor, and had now developed into a powerful and eloquent speaker. No eloquence like his, it is said, had been heard in New England. Multitudes flocked to his preaching wherever it was known he was to be present. He trav-

5

elled extensively in New England, and southerly as far as Pennsylvania, in which missionary tours he gathered multitudes to the Society of Friends. On one occasion there was to be a marriage at the Friends' meeting house in Newport, on a Friday morning. The General Assembly was in session, and adjourned that they might attend it in a body, as they always did to attend the mid-week meeting of Friends. An immense throng crowded the two tiers of gallery and the aisles, and every available spot where there was standing room. The members of the General Assembly came in preceded by their sergeant-at-arms, and took the seats reserved for them, while Governor Wanton, dressed in a bright scarlet cloak, lined with blue,* walked up with great dignity into the minister's gallery, where he took the post of honor.

After a period of silence, customary in gatherings of Friends, the governor arose and quietly stood a few moments with his eyes turned towards heaven; then slowly rolling them downwards towards the

* A piece of this ancient garment is preserved by one of the Wanton family living in Newport.

expectant congregation, he announced for his text,
"There was a narriage in Cana of Galilee and the
nother of Jesus was there." He spoke of the
dignity which was conferred upon the institution of
marriage by the presence of the world's Redeener
on that occasion, and then showed the inportance of
it. First, as a safeguard of norality. Second, as a
school for the culture and developnent of the best
feelings of our nature. Third, as adnirably calcu-
lated for the protection of our race during the help-
less period of infancy; and fourth, as a symbol of
the nysterious union which exists between Christ
and his church. On this latter point he was exceedingly eloquent, and for three-quarters of an hour he
fairly entranced his hearers. Pausing for a noment,
and lowering his voice, he spoke of the superior
adaptation of the cerenony of the Society of Friends
to the fulfillnent of these conditions, and contrasted
it with the cerenony which the British Parlianent
had ordained for the church of England, quoting the
words of the Book of Connon Prayer, "With this
ring I tiee wed; with all ny worldly goods I tiee
endow, and with ny body I thee worsiip." The

governor seized on the latter phrase and played with it as a cat would with a mouse before devouring it. He showed its folly, its absurdity and its wickedness, and wound up with these words: "What! a mortal body worship a mortal body! My friends, it is preposterous!" He uttered these closing words at the very top of his voice, which, ringing through the house, startled the whole congregation, and then quietly took his seat.

During his administration there were certain conflicting Indian claims to be settled within the Colony of Connecticut, and the cause was referred to the governors of Massachusetts, Connecticut and Rhode Island. At this trial the question was agitated whether the sachems should be permitted to speak in their own cause; counsel contended that they should not, and two of the board inclining to that opinion, Governor Wanton remarked, that as they had already agreed to admit the testimony of some of the natives, it would be proper that their chiefs should be allowed to speak. "I have," said he, "been accounted a man of courage in my day, but I think I shall turn coward and flee, if you bring in a body without a head." This sally carried the point, the sachens were allowed to speak, and the governor was often icard to express his admiration of the powers of oratory in those children of the forest.

The public event of greatest importance that occurred during the administration of Governor John Wanton was the declaration of war by Great Britain against Spain, which took place in the spring of 1740, when a special session of the General Assembly was called An act was then passed for raising and enlisting soldiers to be transported to the West Indies for his majesty's service. An officer was accordingly appointed in each militia regiment, who was authorized to enlist as many men as could be found willing to serve the king in an intended expedition against the Spaniards. Every man was to have a bounty of £3 on enlisting, and to be exempt from all military service for the space of three years after his return, except in cases of great extremity. At the same time the Colony was put in a state of defence against an enemy. A garrison under command of Colonel John Cranston was placed in Fort George, and the works put in fight-

ing order. Military stores were provided. Troops
were sent to Block Island, togetier with a battery of
six heavy guns for its defence. Seven watcl : wers
were erected along the coast and on the siores of the
bay, in which the towns where they were located
were to keep a constant guard under the direction of
the council of war. Beacons were also erected upon
conn nanding heigits, including one at Block Island,
to give the earliest notice of any hostile de nonstra-
tion. Furthernore, the Colony ordered the sloop
Tartar, of one hundred and fifteen tons, to be built
for war purposes, and during the coning year five
privateers, manned by four hundred men, were fitted
out by the nerchants of Newport, to cruise against
the Spaniards.

The part tiat Governor Wanton was obliged to
take, by virtue of his office, in the issuing of nili-
tary con nissions and other services connected witi
the war, was a grief to sone of the ultra Friends,
who considered it a breaci of Quaker discipline.
Indeed, it caused suci a con notion tiat a large and
influential con nittee visited iin upon the subject.
He acknowledged his acts, explaining then —

"First: As one of the duties the unfortunate state of the Colony demanded of him in fulfillment of his obligation as the executive of the Colony.

"Second: The duty of the executive to so protect the inhabitants in their rights that they should not be impeded in the exercise of their civil or religious concerns,—the glorious platform of the Colony.

"Third: That he had endeavored, on all previous occasions, as on this, to do his whole duty to God and his fellow-men, without doing violence to the law of conscience, but in all concerns listening to the still small voice of divine emanation, and being obedient thereto."

Before closing this brief sketch of Governors William and John Wanton, it does not seem out of place to mention an amusing incident connected with the first coming of the brothers to Rhode Island, which we have been permitted to take from the unpublished annals of the ancient town of Scituate. Like their father, Edward Wantou, they were both members of the Society of Friends, although they did not inherit his peaceful spirit.

They had long known of the persecutions and exactions of the Presbyterian minister of Scituate, and of the constant annoyances which their father had experienced from this malignant and vindictive man. Often when he sent his colored man to catch a mess of fish, the parson would waylay him and take them from him; Cæsar having been strictly charged never to resist violence. He was constantly circulating the most vile slanders respecting him; he made insulting remarks in his presence, and finally named his dog Wanton. John and William, in obedience to their father's command, had borne all that went before in silence, were now stirred up to ungovernable rage by this last insult. Carefully concealing their project from their father, they had two of his best horses well fed and groomed, and then cut a number of tough willow switches. Thus prepared they waited until ten o'clock in the evening when all the good people were soundly asleep; they then went to the minister's house, and, knocking at the door, the minister came to the window, and asking who was there, was answered, *Friends*. Supposing some couple had come at that late hour to nave the narriage knot tied, he cane down to let then in. When the door was opened they stepped inside and gave him a trenendous whipping with their willow sticks, leaving no whole spot on his skin. His wife attenpted to interfere and call the neighbors, but they very coolly told her that if she stirred or attenpted to screan they would give her a heavy dose of the sane nedicine. When they thougnt his punishnent was about equal to his deserts, tiey gave hin a solenn lecture on the cause of it. They told him they now felt satisfied for all the abuse he had heaped on their father, and were willing to call it even between hin and then.

They gave hin fair warning that if he again repeated any of his inpositions on their father, either by word or deed, they would repeat their punishnent, but with still greater severity. They warned him not to rely upon their father's forbearance, as they had provided certain neans of procuring swift intelligence respecting his conduct, and secret and certain neans of naking him feel their vengeance, though a thousand men were guarding his door.

The minister was very superstitious, and inferred from their language that they had some secret league with the devil. This thoroughly frightened him, and having no desire to be tormented before his time he ever afterwards let Edward Wanton most religiously alone.

On coming out of the house they found Cæsar at the door with two horses, and off they started for Rhode Island, knowing full well that as soon as the whipping was known to the faithful, both Scituate and Plymouth Colony would be too hot to hold them.

The Presbyterians were soon apprized of the punishment which had been inflicted on their minister, when twenty strong fellows, mounted on the best horses they could find, set off in pursuit of the flagellant fugitives.

About three o'clock in the morning, William and John found their horses a good deal blown by the hard pace at which they had travelled, and spying a large tavern with lights in the windows, indicating that the people were awake in the house, they resolved to stop and feed their horses and get some refreshment for themselves.

The pursuing party, after riding a few niles, exchanged horses at a farn house on the road, and had nade a second change just before their arrival at the tavern, thereby enabling then to get over the ground nuci faster than the Wantons. Seeing the lights in the tavern, and feeling pretty sure tiat under suci circunstances a nug of flip was obtainable, tiey all agreed to ialt and refresi thenselves, and at the sane tine nake inquiries in regard to the fugitives.

Just as William and John were getting sonetiing to eat the pursuing party drove up, and leaving their horses tied up in the front, they entered the house. Meanwhile, the Wantons, having discovered their pursuers, rushed out by a back door, and without waiting a nonent, took two of their best iorses and rode off with all speed.

The Presbyterians were not long in following, but the Wantons, iaving a good start of them witi fresi iorses, they could not overtake then. After a long and exciting ciase the pursuers, witi jaded iorses, reluctantly turned back to finisi the flip wiici tiey had but just tasted wien tiey were disturbed by the escape of the young men. Finding the cheer at the tavern pretty good, they resolved to repay themselves for their failure to catch the runaways by having a good time. They remained there all that day and night, and the next morning rode home and gave the people of Scituate a fearful account of their hardships, and received credit among their neighbors for having ridden incessantly for thirty-six hours.

When the Wantons arrived at Fall River their minds were relieved. Here they rested themselves and their horses, and on the next day reached Newport in safety.

But Governor Wanton was not permitted to perfect his schemes for carrying on the war with Spain. He had been annually re-elected to the office of governor for seven years, or until 1742, when he died on the 5th May of that year. He was laid in the Coddington burial ground, where a marble monument marks his resting place. His portrait in the State House in Providence, which was taken in early life, shows him to have been a man of middling stature, thin features and of fair complexion.

JOHN WANTON, eldest son of Governor John, born 22nd tenth month, 1697, had the following children,* as appears from his family Bible: 1. Mehitable,˙ born September 6, 1719; 2. Edward, born April 8, 1721; 3. John, born January 1, 1723; 4. Ann, born July 25, 1728; 5. William, born March 9, 1730; 6. second Mehitable, November 1, 1732; 7. second Edward, September 9,.1733; 8. Mary, born January 10, 1736; 9. third Mehitable, born March 8, 1738, and died at Boston, December 1, 1839, aged one hundred and one years; 10. Jonas Langford, born May 25, 1740, died November 30, 1827, at Cranston, aged eighty-seven, and left no children; 11. Sarah, born May 3, 1742, who married Lathan Thurston, February 4, 1768.

Of the children of Elizabeth Wanton, born in 1700, who married John Cupitt; of Susanna, born in 1704, died in 1740, who married Joseph Slocum; and Mary, born in 1707, died 1737, who married

* Mr. Savage, in his Genealogical Dictionary, (volume iv., page 406,) makes an error in giving the names of the children of Governor John Wanton. The names he gives are those of the children of Joseph, the first son of Edward, who married the daughter of Gideon Freeborn.

Lathan Thurston, I have no knowledge. Their names do not appear in the family Bible.

JAMES WANTON, the youngest son of Governor John W., born the 16th of the seventh month (July or September), 1717, married Patience ——, August 6, 1741, and had the following children, as appears by the family Bible: 1. Rebecca, born March 21, 1746. 2. John, born January 19, ——; 3. James, born June 12, 1750; 4. Mary, born June 15, 1753, died July 17, same year; 5. George, born June 9, 1755; 6. Hannah, born May 22, 175—; 7. Mary, born February 23, 1761, and 8. Benjamin, born March 11, 1763, died September 14, 1765.

MICHAEL WANTON, the ninth child of Edward Wanton, was born in 1673, and settled on the paternal estate in Scituate, Massachusetts. His marriage to Mary Mew of Scituate, the 15th of eleventh month, 1704, is on the town records; but she was born in Newport. He was a man of meek and quiet spirit, on whose shoulders the spiritual mantle of his father descended, succeeding him as a religious teacher of the Society of Friends, in Scituate. He inherited his father's homestead, his ship-yards, his business, and a very considerable portion of his personal estate. His business faculties were very good, and he greatly augmented the estate which he inherited. His children were: Ruth, born in 1705; Mary, born in 1707; Stephen, born in 1709. Mary Mew died 22nd fifth month, 1711. On the 2nd of eleventh month, 1717, Michael married, for his second wife, Abigail Carr, widow of William Carr, of Jamestown. She was the daughter of Robert Barker, of Penbroke, and returned there after she became a widow. The children of Michael and Abigail were Susannah, born 1717; Hannah, born 1721, and Michael, born 1724. We learn from letters preserved in the family that Michael Wanton travelled much on missionary tours, and was a successful and beloved minister. He did not possess the fiery eloquence of his father, but there was a vein of solemn and instructive thought, and a spirit of pure, loving zeal for the truth running through his discourses that greatly tended to build up his hearers in their most holy faith. Indeed, it was said that, "although there was not so great an increase in numbers during his ministry as under that of his father, yet the members were in a much better spiritual condition. They could give a better reason for the faith that was in them, and they abounded more in love and in good works."

Mary, second daughter of Michael Wanton, born 1707, married Daniel Coggeshall of Portsmouth, July 27, 1726, whose daughter Abigail, born February 14, 1737, married Silas Casey, of East Greenwich, ancestor of Major General Casey, U. S. Army.

Stephen Wanton, son of Michael, born 1709, inherited the family estate, which he sold to John Stetson in 1740, and removed to Newport, where he died in 1760, aged 56 years. He married Mary, daughter of Samuel Clarke, of Conanicut, sister of Joseph Clarke, General Treasurer, April 7, 1736, by whom he had the following children: 1. Michael, born 1740, died June 13, 1756; 2. Samuel, born May 1, 1743, died June 16, 1744; 3. Hannah,* born 1747, who married James Gould, December 7, 1780, and died April 1, 1831, aged 84 years; 4. Mary,

*See appendix for genealogy of Gould family.

born 1752, died May 4, 1818, aged 67; 5. Ruth, born April 16, 1753, died May 22, 1756; 6. Martha, born 1758, married Capt. John Stanton, and died May 20, 1836, aged 78 years.

Stephen Wanton was brought up in his father's business of ship-building, but having different tastes took no active part in it. He had a fine education and was of a studious turn, but had no taste for politics. His conversational powers were of a high order; these, with his courtly and agreeable manner, gave him a fine position in the social circle.

In 1739 he removed to Newport, and with capital furnished by his grandfather Clarke, and his uncles William and John, he entered into the West India trade, in which he employed many ships. Two years later his father, Michael, died, when he inherited one-third his fortune. He now sold his ship-yard, and gave his whole attention to commerce. His business was large; indeed, at this time, the commerce of Newport is said to have been equal to that of New York. After a few years, Stephen Wanton found his fortune had so much increased that he said " more would be a burden" to him; he, therefore, retired from business altogether, relinquishing it in favor of his two nephews, sons of his sister, Ruth Freeborn, who had been brought up in his counting-room. Newport, even at this early date, was a favorite resort for intellectual and wealthy families from England. Officers of the British Navy, travellers and Huguenot refugees also resorted here, so that the society was the most refined and intelligent then to be found in the British colonies.

STEPHEN WANTON, tenth child of the first Edward, born in 1682, lived and died in Newport, leaving no children.

PHILIP WANTON, eleventh and youngest child of the first Edward, was born in 1686, lived in Newport, and united the business of merchant and apothecary. He married Hannah, daughter of Thomas and Hannah (Clarke) Rodman, October 31, 1711. He died in 1735, and was buried in the Clifton Burial Ground. His children were: 1. Walter, born November 27, 1712; 2. Hannah, born July 15, 1715, married, March 15, 1737, Latham Stanton, who died October 4, 1757; 3. Philip, born May 31, 1719;

4. Thomas, born March 14, 1722; 5. Mary, born
March 29, 1725, married Thomas Borden, November 3, 1748; 6. Elizabeth, born (probably 1727),
married William, son of William and Abigail Robinson, May 17, 1750.

PHILIP WANTON, third son of Philip and grandson
of the first Edward, was born May 31, 1719. He
succeeded to his father's business of a merchant and
apothecary, and married (1.) Elizabeth Casey,
daughter of John and Elizabeth (Hicks) Casey, of
Newport, December 28, 1748. She died June 25,
1757, aged 35 years. (2.) Sarah Lawton, widow,
May 28, 1761; who died January 1796. By his first
wife he had Elizabeth, born October 28, 1756. By his
second wife, Philip, born April 1, 1762, who moved
to Alexandria, Va., in 1790; Hannah, born April
30, 1763, died May 3, 1794; Sarah, born Nov. 22,
1764; Mary, born September 18, 1766, and Walter
Clarke, born July 15, 1768, and died at sea.

PHILIP WANTON, of Alexandria, Virginia, third
son of the last-named Philip, and great-grandson of
the first Edward, was born April 1, 1762, and died

February 27, 1832. He married Mary (Pancoast)
Saunders, widow of John Saunders, of Philadelphia,
May 31, 1792. She was born in 1762, and died
November 26, 1846, aged 84 years. They had the
following children: 1. Hannah Shreeves, born April
1, 1793, died August 11, 1794; 2. Hannah Shreeves,
born August 10, 1795, died Oct. 13, 1860, unmarried; 3. William Rodman, born March 27, 1798, died
September 7, 1849; 4. Elizabeth Pancoast, born
August 27, 1800, died September 6, 1803; 5. Mary
Hewes,* born March 1, 1803, married John Richardson Pierpont, September 26, 1833, died October 15,
1876.

WILLIAM RODMAN WANTON, of Alexandria, son
of the foregoing Philip, born March 27, 1798, married Mary Elizabeth Hewes, born in 1813 and died
in Washington, D. C., December 27, 1876, aged 63

*MARY HEWES WANTON, born March 1, 1803, died Oct. 15, 1876, married
Sept. 6, 1833, John Richardson Pierpont, of Obed, from Loudon County,
Virginia, who was born Nov. 15, 1799. Their children were: 1. A daugh-
ter born January 1, 1835, died in infancy; 2. William Wanton Pierpont,
born March, 1836, died Aug. 10, 1842; 3. John Edwin Pierpont, born
March 23, 1841.

years. He died Septenber 7, 1849. Tiey had the following children: 1. William Rodnan, born —— died 1872; 2. Julia; 3. Mary; 4. Hannaı; 5. John; 6. Virginia.

Governor GIDEON WANTON, son of Joseph, of Tiverton, grandson of the first Edward, and nephew of William and John, was the tiird Governor of the Wanton nane. He was born October 20, 1693; narried Mrs. Mary Codnan, February 6, 1718, and died Septenber 12, 1767, at the age of 74. His wife died Septenber 3, 1780, at the age of 87, and was laid in the Friends' Burial Ground, Newport. His children were: 1. Gideon, Jr.; 2. John G., born in 1729; 3. Joseph, Jr., born February 8, 1730, and 4. Edward. The ıouse wıere he lived, in Broad street, Newport, is occupied by Mrs. Benjamin Hazard, a descendant.

Gideon Wanton held the office of General Treasurer fron 1733 to 1743, and two years later was chosen Governor, succeeding William Greene. He ıeld the office one year, and in 1747 was again cıosen for one year. Two of his sons, Joın and

Gideon, Jr., were long in public life. Both were
members of the General Assembly when the Declaration of Independence was ratified by the State.

Shortly before Gideon Wanton came into office,
war had broken out anew between Great Britain and
France, and the former was devising plans to drive
the French from Canada. A pressing letter was
received by his predecessor from the Duke of Newcastle, calling upon him to furnish men, provisions
and shipping to Commodore Warren, who was then
engaged in fitting out an expedition against the
French.

A letter was also received from Gov. Shirley of
Massachusetts, a few days after Gideon Wanton had
been installed as Governor, calling for assistance in
raising troops for the expedition against Cape Breton.
This was followed by others more pressing, calling
for seamen for manning the ship Vigilant, which had
been captured by Commodore Warren from the
French. In one of these letters Governor Shirley
says that he has issued his warrants for impressing
seamen, but finds his " endeavors to be of little purpose, as all mariners subject to impressment fly to

Rhode Island to avoid it, and are tiere sheltered and encouraged, when tiere are nany iundreds of foreign seanen walking the streets of Newport, wiile scarce one is to be found in Boston." He then urges Governor Wanton to exert iinself to secure the seanen wanted, wiici he tiinks may be accon- plished either by offering a bounty to volunteers, or by inpressing.

The taking of Louisburg by the Englisi forces, in which both Aassachusetts and Rhode Island took part, is an event well known in history. In order to keep possession of this place, whici was spoken of by Sir Peter Warren, the officer connanding the English fleet, as "the key to all the Frenci settle- nents upon the continent," that officer wrote to Governor Wanton for assistance. He asked for soldiers for the garrison, arned and victualed for seven or eigit nonths. The people of Riode Island were invited to Louisburg to trade, and, as an addi- tional inducenent, Sir Peter writes tiat "tiere are several Frenci prizes iere, wiici will be condenned and disposed of, and many more will, no doubt, fall into our hands daily, by our cruisers." Governor

Shirley at the same time called upon Governor Wanton to furnish gunpowder, of which there was a short supply at Louisburg. He adds, "I must desire your Honor to lay an embargo upon all the powder now lying in your stores or magazines (as I have done for several months past in Massachusetts) so as to secure it for the service of the expedition against Cape Breton, at the market price."

The General Assembly had voted to raise two hundred men for the Canada expedition. Governor Shirley acknowledges the arrival of seventy-five of these for the ship Vigilant, and urges Governor Wanton to raise more landsmen, "as there is great danger of Louisburg's being snatched from us, before his majesty shall garrison it, and the fortifications be repaired." A few days later, Commodore Warren wrote to Governor Wanton that his squadron had taken a rich East India ship, whose cargo would be sold, and invited the merchants of Rhode Island to come and make purchases.

The sloop Tartar, which had been built in Rhode Island and placed under command of Captain Fones, reached Louisburg in safety, and joined the squadron

under Conmodore Warren. In a letter fron Captain
Fones to Governor Wanton he says: " I now have
the pleasure of walking Louisburg streets, which is
the strongest place I ever saw; ny people are all
alive and nost of then well."

General Sir William Pepperell, who connanded
the New England troops at the taking of Louisburg,
wrote to Governor Wanton, congratulating hin and
the people of Rhode Island for the success of his
najesty's army. "The three conpanies," writes Sir
William, " raised in your Colony for our assistance,
with connission fron you, arrived here last week,
and you may be assured shall have ny favor and
countenance in everything in ny power." He states
that a large stock of provisions and warlike stores
for the army, to be laid in before the fall, are necessary. That there should be provisions for three
thousand or four thousand men, for twelve or fifteen
nonths, and he further urges Governor Wanton to
render all the aid in his power, in order that the
place may be prevented from falling into the hands
of the French again. He also speaks of the capture
of a second French vessel, " a vastly rich South Sea-

man." Governor Phipps, of Massachusetts, also writes about the prize, which he says was taken within sight of the garrison, and "had £400,000 pounds in money, besides a valuable cargo of merchandise." He estimated the value of the captures, with cost of French ships, to be nearly £1,000,000 sterling.

Governor Phipps calls upon Governor Wanton for farther aid. " Massachusetts," he says, " is exhausted of men, provisions, clothing, ammunition and other things necessary for the support of the garrison at Louisburg." Not only these are wanted, but money also. Massachusetts had also contributed largely in money for the expedition, and Governor Phipps thinks the other provinces should not object to subjecting themselves to the charge of a few thousand pounds. "For if the place should be recovered by the French, for want of sufficient strength to hold it, the blame must lie upon the colonies that refuse to bear their part in the charge and dangers of this important enterprise."

To those now living it may seem singular that so great a power as Great Britain should have called

upon this little Colony for such a number of men,
with provisions and shipping, to aid in the conquest
of Canada; but she knew that her New England
colonists had accomplished much in the frontier
wars, and had been equally successful on the high
seas; besides, they were near the field of operations,
and could reach there in a few days. Massachusetts
had always led the way with men, money and ships,
in defence of her mother country, and Rhode Island
had only been second to her in numbers. In privateers, the latter had furnished more than the other
colonies, and some were so jealous of her promi-
nence at sea that her leading commercial men were
charged with being in complicity with the pirates, of
which there were such numbers on our coast and
among the West India Islands.

The correspondence between Governor Wanton,
the Duke of Newcastle, Governor Shirley, Admiral
Warren, Sir William Pepperell,* Sir William Phipps

---

* Sir William Pepperell was an American merchant, living in the
Province of Maine. About the year 1727 he was chosen a member of
his majesty's council, of the Province of Massachusetts, to which he
was annually elected until his death, a period of thirty-two years. He
commanded the expedition against Louisburg, at the time of its capit-

and Richard Partridge, the agent for Rhode Island
in London, is of great interest, but too voluninous
for a place in tis sketch.   It is evident, however,
fron Governor Wanton's letters, that, although a
Quaker, he was a belligerent one, and fully equal to
the energency; and had he been governor and captain general of Rhode Island in 1861, would have
been anong the first to send a reginent of Riode
Island volunteers to Washington.   Through life
Gideon Wanton was distinguished for his talents and
for the influence he exerted in the affairs of the Colony.   Unfortunately, no portrait of hin renains.

JOHN G. WANTON, son of Governor Gideon Wanton, born in 1729, was nnch in public life, and was
one of the corporators of Rhode Island College, in
1764.   He becane a distinguished nerchant of Newport during the Revolutionary war.   He narried,
first, Abigail Robinson, of Soutı Cingstown, Octo-

ulation.   After this achievement he went to England, where he
received a first coloneley in the army; in 1755, the rank of major-general; and two years later, that of lieutenant general.   He was also
rewarded with the dignity of baronet and the thanks of the ministry.
An exhaustive memoir of him was written by Dr. Usher Parsons, of
Providence, R. I., and published in 1855.

ber 5, 1752. She died March 3, 1754, aged twenty-three years, and was buried on the estate, now (1878) belonging to the Hon. William Sprague. His second wife was Mary, daughter of Governor Henry Bull, whom he married in 1760. He died July 2, 1799, aged sixty-eight years. Dean Berkeley, who was the friend of Mr. Wanton, stood godfather to Mary Bull when she was christened; and, always proud of this distinction, the latter kept a copy of his "Minute Philosopher" in her posession as long as she lived. Mary Bull Wanton died, at Newport, March 12, 1821, aged ninety-two years and ten months.

The children of John G. and Mary (Bull) Wanton were Mary, born August 20, 1763, and Gideon, born July 19, 1766. The latter died, in Newport, November 27, 1786.

Upon the arrival of the French fleet at Newport, in 1780, Mr. Wanton received and entertained the officers at his house with great hospitality; and it was on this occasion that Major Daniel Lyman, aid to General Heath, who was deputed to welcome the French, first saw Mary Wanton, whom he after-

wards narried. Later, the najor became Chief Jus-
of the Suprene Court of Rhode Island.*

Governor JOSEPH WANTON, son of Governor
Willian Wanton, was born August 15, 1705. Like
his father before 1in, he adhered to the Church of
England. He narried Mary, daughter of John Still
Winthrop, of New London, and had the following
children : 1. Joseph, born 1730 ; 2. William, who
was collector of custons at St. John, New Bruns-
wick ; 3. John, who died young ; 4. Catherine, who
narried, first, Robert Stoddard, November 29, 1767,
second, Dr. Destailleur, a surgeon in the British
arny ; 5. Mary, who narried Captain John Coddington, of Newport, January 28, 1759 ; 6. Elizabeth, who narried, in 1762, Thonas Wickhan, of
Newport, whose descendants live in Western New
York ; 7. Ruth, who narried William Browne, Governor of Bernuda ; and 8. Ann, born March, 1734,
who narried her cousin, Winthrop Saltonstall of
New London, son of General Gurdon S. and grandson of Governor Saltonstall, April 17, 1763, and
had five children. She died in 1784. See Appendix for descendants.

* For notice of the descendants of Judge Lyman, see appendix.

Joseph was an opulent merchant of Newport and connected by blood and affinity with the wealthiest and most prominent families in the Colony. His portrait, evidently an original, in the Redwood Library at Newport, and of which a copy has been made for the State House in Providence, shows him to have been a remarkably handsome man. He was called one of the most courtly gentlemen in the Colony; of pleasing manners and cultivated tastes.

In his "History of the Narragansett Church," Mr. Updike says that this Joseph was, in 1764 and 1767, elected deputy governor through the Hopkins influence. This is evidently incorrect, as there was a Joseph Wanton, Jr., son of Governor Joseph, who had been for many years a member of the General Assembly, and who, it is believed, was the deputy governor. There is a letter (see Peterson's Rhode Island, page 209) from Stephen Hopkins to the people of the State, dated April 16, 1764, in praise of the character of the Mr. Wanton who was deputy governor under him, in which he says, "he is but a boy about thirty-four years old." Now, Governor Joseph Wanton, being born in 1705, was then fifty-nine years of age, which clearly shows that he was not the deputy governor, as supposed.

There has been a question who the Joseph Wanton, Jr., was, who was lieutenant governor in 1764-1767, as Governor Gideon Wanton had a son, Joseph, born in 1730. In the record of births, at Newport, is the name of Joseph Wanton, born 1730. (His father's name is not stated.) Now, Governor Joseph, who was born in 1705 had a son named Joseph, who was his eldest child. We find, too, that by the records of Harvard College, Joseph Wanton, Jr., born February 8, 1730, entered college at sixteen and a half years of age. Again, Mr. Hopkins, in 1764, says, the Mr. Wanton who was elected deputy governor, was thirty-four years old. All these, evidently, refer to the same individual, and show that it was the son of Governor Joseph who was the deputy governor under Hopkins, and, furthermore, that he, and not Governor Joseph, as has been supposed, was the graduate of Harvard. *

*On the 3d of June, 1771, George Bissett preached a sermon in Trinity Church, Newport, "at the funeral of Mrs. Abigail Wanton, late consort of the Honorable Joseph Wanton, Jr., who died on the 31st of

Joseph Wanton was elected governor of Rhode Island, in 1769, succeeding Governor Lyndon.

An important event, in the history of the Colony, occurred at Newport, in July, following the installation of Governor Wanton into office. It may, indeed, be called the first open resistance, in the colonies, against the acts of the British government, which led to their final separation from the mother country.

It appears that a revenue vessel, called the Liberty, commanded by Captain Reid, had been fitted out by the commissioners of the King's revenue or customs, at Boston, and sent to the waters of Rhode

---

May, in the thirty-sixth year of her age." This lady was, doubtless, the first wife of the deputy governor.

Rivington's [New York] *Royal Gazette* of August 9, 1780, has the following notice, which, we think, refers to the same individual: "It is with inexpressible sorrow we announce to the public that yesterday morning, at 7 o'clock, departed this life, the Honorable Joseph Wanton, Jr., Esq , superintendent general of the police of Rhode Island. The extreme distress in which the friends of this gentleman are involved by so melancholy an event will only admit them to say, that his funeral will proceed this afternoon from the quarters of Major John Morrison, deputy commissary general, in Malden Lane, and that they request his acquaintances in this city, as well as the Loyalists from the different colonies, will attend the same, as the last office they can perform to the memory of their friend."

Island, to detain and examine all vessels suspected of violating the revenue laws. This vessel took a brig and sloop, belonging to Connecticut, which she brought into Newport. Here some difficulties took place, and for some slight provocation, the captain of the brig was fired on by those on board the Liberty. Obtaining no redress for this outrage, a party, said to have been chiefly from Connecticut, boarded the obnoxious vessel, cut her cables, and suffered her to drift on shore near Long Wharf. They then cut away her masts, threw her armament overboard, when she drifted on to Goat Island. The first night she lay here, a party went over from Newport and burned her. Her boats were run up Long Wharf, thence up the parade, and through Broad street by the populace and burned.

The provocation which led to the firing, is thus given in the Providence *Gazette* of July 22, 1769.

"The captain of the brig, it appears, went on board his vessel for some linen and clothes, when he was informed that they had been removed on board the Liberty. On enquiring for his sword, he was told that it was in the cabin, where a man lay on it. Ho

went below to get it, wien he was accosted by oat is
and inprecations. He then seized his sword, wiici
the sloop's men endeavored to take fron hin, but
failed to do so; and getting into his boat, set out for
the shore. The revenue sloop was tien iailed and
infor ned of what had taken place, when she fired on
the boat, which proceedings were witnessed by people on the wharf."

As Captain Reid had not siown his con nission to
Governor Wanton, the people obliged iin to order
his men on shore, in order to discover who had fired
on Captain Packwood.

Tiis event, witi attenpts by the colonists to
evade the custom duties, led to a correspondence
between Governor Wanton and the Earl of Hillsborough, in whici the latter conplained tiat "the
officers of the custons iave received no support or
countenance from the governnent of Riode Island,
and iave, in vain, applied to the superior court for
writs of assistance in cases where suci writs were
judged necessary." In conclusion, Lord Hillsborough says: "Any further exiortation on tiat subject
would be useless; and it must remain with tiose to

wɪoɴ the powers of governɴeɴt in Rɪode Island are entrusted to consider what ɴust be the consequence, if, after such repeated adɴoɴitions, the laws of the kingdoɴ are suffered to be traɴpled upon, and violences and outrages of so reprehensible a nature are coɴɴitted with inpunity."

Governor Wanton, in his reply to the Earɪ of Hillsborough, under date of Noveɴber 2, 1771, enters into an explanation of the charges against the Colony, and, with regard to the latter charge, says:

"As to that part of the coɴplaint against the superior court, for refusing writs of assistance, the General Asseɴbly, willing to know the truth of tɪat ɴatter, called the justices of the superior court before theɴ, to give account of what applications had been made to theɴ for writs of assistance, and what was the occasion they refused to give the officers of the custoɴs that protection the law required them to give; that all the justices of the superior court declared, upon their ɪonors, to the Asseɴbly, tɪat no kind of application, whatsoever, had been ɴade to theɴ, or any of theɴ by any of the officers of the customs, for any writ of assistance or otɪer protection of any kind, for several years past; and the justices of the Superior Court further said, that when any application should be made to them, by the custom house officers for writs of assistance or other protection, they would readily give them every assistance in the execution of their duty which the law put it in the power of the court to give."

"And now, my Lord," continues Governor Wanton, "permit me, in my turn, to complain of the officers of his majesty's customs, in America, for their abusing and misrepresenting the Colony of Rhode Island and its officers; for how unkind and ungentlemanly-like it is for officers, sent abroad by the crown to reside in the colonies, by every means in their power to traduce and even falsely accuse his majesty's faithful subjects of this Colony to their sovereign and his ministers of state."

"I am now to thank your Lordship for the kind concern you are pleased to express for the Colony and its safety, and hope that your Lordship will transfer your reprehensions from the innocent Colony of Rhode Island to those guilty officers who have so shamefully misinformed you in all those matters contained in your Lordship's letter."

I am Sir, &c., &c.,

JOSEPH WANTON.

To the Right Honorable the
    EARL OF HILLSBOROUGH.

In March, 1772, the British armed schooner Gaspee, of eight guns, Lieutenant Dudingston, accompanied by the Beaver, made their appearance in the waters of Narragansett Bay, on duties similar to those of the "Liberty," to which allusion has been made, viz. : to prevent breaches of the revenue laws, and to stop the illicit trade, carried on in the Colony. The commander of the Gaspee was quite as exacting as Captain Reid of the Liberty had been. He stopped all vessels, including small market boats, without showing his authority for so doing; and even sent the goods he had illegally siezed to Boston for trial, contrary to an act of Parliament, which required such trials to be held in the colonies where the seizures were made. In these acts Dudingston clearly transcended his powers. The complaints from the people of Providence against him became so numerous that Deputy Governor Sessions submitted the question to Chief Justice Stephen Hopkins. The latter promptly gave his opinion, "that no commander of any vessel has a right to use any authority in the body of the Colony, without previously applying to the Governor, and showing

his warrant for so doing; and also being sworn to a
due exercise of his office."

Deputy Governor Sessions, who resided in Providence, at once wrote to Governor Wanton, apprising
i in of what had taken place, and tiat it was the
opinion of the Chief Justice that the acts of the connander of the Gaspee were illegal.

Governor Wanton now sent a note, by the hands
of the High Sheriff, to Lieutenant Dudingston, under
date of the 22nd March, 1772, calling his attention
to complaints against his "searching and detaining
every little packet boat plying between the several
towns." "You are requested," writes the Governor,
"without delay, to produce your connission and
instructions, if any you have, which was your duty
to have done when you first cane within the jurisdic-
tion of the Colony." The following day Dudingston
replied to Governor Wantou, saying that he had
done nothing but what was his duty. "When I
waited on you," writes the officer, "I acquainted you
of ny being sent to this government to assist the
revenue. I had ny connission to show you, if
required, as it was even understood by all his majes-

ty's governors I have had the honor to wait on, that every officer commanding one of his majesty's vessels was propely authorized, and never did produce it unasked for." The Governor replied the same day to Lieutenant Dudingston, telling him his answer did not give him "the satisfaction he had a right to expect," and again asked him to conply with his (the Governor's) request of the previous day.

The lieutenant's sense of propriety was evidently shocked by the governor's letters, and his peremptory demand to exhibit his connission and instructions. He, therefore, enclosed the correspondence to Adniral Montagu, connanding his najesty's fleet at Boston. The adniral espoused the side of Dudingston and dispatched the following letter to Governor Wanton:

BOSTON, 8th April, 1772.

"SIR:—Lieutenant Dudingston, connander of his najesty's arned schooner, and a part of the squadron under ny connand, has sent me two letters he received fron you, of such a nature that I am at a loss what answer to give then, and ashaned to find they cane fron one of his najesty's governors. He

inforns me tiat he waited upon you, and showed
you the admiralty and otier orders for his proceedings; which, agreeable to his instructions, he is to
do, that you may be acquainted he is on that station
to protect your province from pirates and give the
tiade all the assistance he can, and to endeavor, as
much as lays in his power, to protect the revenue
officer, and to prevent (if possible) the illicit trade
that is carrying on in Rhode Island.

" He, sir, has done his duty, and behaved like an
officer; and it is your duty, as a governor, to give
hin your assistance, and not endeavor to distress the
king's officers, for strictly conplying with ny orders.
I shall give them directions, that, in case they receive
any nolestation in the execution of their duty, tiat
they shall send every man so taken in nolesting
then to me.   I am also inforned, the people of
Newport talk of fitting out an arned vessel to rescue
any vessel the king's schooner may take carrying on
an illicit trade.   Let then be cautious what they do;
for as sure as they attenpt it, and any of tien are
taken, I will hang tien as pirates.   I shall report
your two insolent letters to ny officer, to his najesty's secretaries of state, and leave then to deternine
what right you have to denand a sight of all orders
I shall give to ny squadron; and I would advise you
not to send your sheriff on board the king's ship

again, on such ridiculous errands. The captains and
lieutenants have all ny orders, to give you assistance whenever you denand it; but further, you have
no business with then; and be assured, it is not
their duty to show you any part of ny orders or
instructions to then."   •

I am, Sir. &c., &c.,

J. MONTAGU.

To Governor Wanton.

Governor Wanton submitted this renarkable letter
to the General Assembly, at its May session. He
also submitted a draught of his own in reply, whereupon a resolution of approval was adopted, and the
Governor was requested to transnit the letter to Admiral Montagu. He was further requested to transmit
to the Earl of Hillsborough, secretary of state, a
narrative containing all the proceedings referred to
in the letter, together with a copy of the admiral's
letter to him and his answer to the same.

Governor Wanton's Letter to Admiral Montagu.

RHODE ISLAND, May 8, 1772.

SIR:—" Your letter, dated April the 8th, at Boston, I have received. Lieutenant Dudingston has done
well in transnitting ny letters to you, which I sent

hin ; but I am sorry to be inforned there is any thing contained in then that should be construed as a design of giving offence, when no such thing was intended. But Mr. Dudingston has not behaved so well, in asserting to you, 'he waited on me, and showed me the adniralty and your orders for his proceedings, which, agreeably to his instructions, he is to do'; but in that he has altogether nisinforned you ; for he, at no tine, ever showed me any orders fron the adniralty, or from you ; and positively denied that he derived any authority either fron you or the con nissioners ; therefore, it was altogether out of ny power to know, whether he cane hither to protect us fron pirates or was. pirate hinself. You say, 'he has done his duty and behaved like an officer.' In this, I apprehend, you nust be nistaken ; for I never can believe it is the duty of an officer to give false infornation for his superiors. As to your attenpt to point out what was ny duty as governor, please to be inforned, that I do not receive instructions for the adninistration of my governnent fron the king's adniral stationed in Anerica.

"You seen to assert, that I have endeavored to distress the king's officers, for strictly conplying with your orders. In this, you are altogether mistaken ; for I have at all tines, heretofore, and shall, constantly, for tine to cone, afford tien all the aid and assistance in my power in the execution of ny office.

*　　*　　*　　*　　*　　*　　*　　*　　*

"I am greatly obliged to you for the pronise of transnitting ny letters to the secretary of state. I am, however, a little shocked at your inpolite expression, nade use of upon that occasion. In return for tiis good office, I shall also transnit your letter to the secretary of state, and leave to the king and his ninisters to deternine on wiich side the charge of insolence lies. As to your advice, not to send the sheriff on board any of your squadron, please to know that I will send the sheriff of this Colony at any tine, and to any place within the body of it, as I shall think fit.

"In the last paragraph of your letter, you are pleased, flatly, to contradict what you wrote in the beginning; for there you assert that Dudingston, by his instructions, was directed to siow me the admiralty and your orders to 1in; and here you assert, that I have no business with tien; and assure me that it is not his duty to show me then, or any part thereof."

I am, Sir, &c., &c.,

J. WANTON.

To Admiral Montagu.

The foregoing letters present an account of the events which preceded the nenorable nigit of the

9th of June, when the Gaspee was destroyed. That Dudingston did not act wisely, to say the least, in exerting the authority he did, without first exhibiting his connission, is evident. But it is certain, that in sending property seized by him within the County of Kent in Rhode Island, to Boston for adjudication, he was clearly in the wrong; as an act of parliament expressly declares that such seizures shall be adjudicated in the colony where the seizure is made. Dudingston seens to have been aware that this act was illegal, as he did not dare to venture on shore, having been threatened with a suit at law by the Messrs. Greene of East Greenwich, the owners of the goods seized.

As the most important event that took place during the administration of Joseph Wanton was the burning of the Gaspee, and his correspondence and action, connected with it, both before and subsequent to it, a brief account of it seens necessary.

The appearance of this British war vessel, under the connand of Lieutenant Dudingston, had given great offence to the merchants of Newport and Providence by stopping all vessels, large and snall, entering or

leaving any of the ports on the siores of Narragansett Bay. On the 9th of June, Captain Lindsey left
Newport in his packet for Providence, followed by
the Gaspee, for the purpose of examining her cargo.
In this pursuit the Gaspee ran aground near Nam-
quit Point, about seven niles below Providence.
Lindsey continued up the bay and reached Providence about sunset, and lost no tine in naking
known to Ar. John Brown, one of the nost respect-
able nerchants, the situation of the Gaspee.

Ar. Brown, at once. resolved on the destruction
of the schooner; to acconplish wiich, he directed
one of his nost trusty ship-nasters to collect eight
of the largest long-boats in the harbor, and have
their oars muttled, to prevent noise. Early in the
evening a man passed througi Aain street, beating
a drun to attract the attention of the iniabitants,
whon he infor ned that the Gaspee was aground.
He, furthernore, invited all who felt disposed to
take part in an expedition to destroy the vessel, to
meet at a place appointed, where boats would be in
readiness to receive tien. The party accordingly
assenbled and enbarked in the boats provided for

the purpose. Captain Abraham Whipple and Captain John B. Hopkins, son of Connodore Esek Hopkins, directed the boats. When about sixty yards from the Gaspee they were hailed by a sentinel, but nade no reply. Dudingston, himself, next hailed the boats, when a shot was fired at him, which took effect. The next ninute the vessel was boarded without opposition, Dudingston and his men retreating to the cabin. The wounded officer was carefully attended by Dr. John Mawney, a young surgeon who happened to be one of the attacking party; after which he and his crew were put into boats, with their clothing and other effects, and sent on shore at Pawtuxet. The schooner was then set on fire and destroyed. As soon as Deputy Governor Sessions heard of the affair, he sought the wounded officer, on whom he bestowed every attention, providing the best surgical aid and doing all in his power to adninister to his conforts.

As night be supposed, this bold affair created a great sensation throughout the British colonies. Governor Wanton issued a proclanation, offering a reward for the discovery of the offenders, and wrote a letter to the Earl of Hillsborough, giving full particulars of the events which preceded the destruction of the vessel, as well as all the facts that could be collected regarding the transaction itself; promising "that the utmost vigilance of the civil authority should be employed to bring the perpetrators to exemplary and condign punishment."

As soon as the news of the destruction of the Gaspee reached England, the king issued his proclamation, which was published in the Colony, offering a reward of £500 for such information as would lead to the discovery and conviction of the perpetrators of the crime.

The king appointed a royal commission of enquiry to investigate the affair. This commission, which met at Newport, on the 5th of January, 1773, consisted of Governor Wanton, Daniel Horsmanden, chief justice of the Province of New York; Frederic Snyth, chief justice of New Jersey; Peter Oliver, chief justice of Massachusetts Bay; and Robert Auchmuty, judge of the Vice Admiralty Court, Boston.

The meeting of the royal commission, and its pro-

ceedings, which were printed in the Boston newspapers, attracted great attention throughout the colonies; and, although a large number of witnesses
were examined, and every effort, apparently, made
to discover the parties engaged in the destruction of
the Gaspee, they were never discovered.

Joseph Wanton was annually elected to the office
of Governor until 1775; his last election occurring
on the third Wednesday in April of that year. A
few days later (April 22d), in consequence of the
passage of the Boston Port Bill, the General Assembly was specially convened at Providence. But the
newly elected governor and other colonial officers
could not be sworn into office until the regular meeting of the General Assembly, on the first day of
May ensuing. Meanwhile the battle of Lexington
had been fought, and the people of the Colony,
determined on immediate action, passed, at its April
session, the following preamble and resolution:

"At this very dangerous crisis of American affairs,
at a time when we are surrounded with fleets and ·
armies which threaten our immediate destruction;
at a time when fear and anxieties of the people

9

throw them into the utmost distress, and totally prevent them from attending the common occupations of life; to prevent the mischievous consequences that must necessarily attend such a disordered state, and to restore peace to the minds of the good people of this Colony, it appears absolutely necessary to this Assembly that a number of men be raised and embodied, properly armed and disciplined, to continue in this Colony as an army of observation, to repel any insult or violence that may be offered to the inhabitants; and also, if it be necessary for the safety and preservation of any of the colonies, to march out of this Colony and join and co-operate with the forces of the neighboring colonies. It is therefore voted and resolved, that fifteen hundred men be enlisted, raised and embodied, as aforesaid, with all the expedition and dispatch that the nature of things will admit of."

To this resolution, Governor Wanton and several of the assistants made the following protest:

"We, the subscribers, professing true allegiance to his majesty King George the Third, beg leave to dissent from the vote of the House of Magistrates, for enlisting, raising and embodying an army of observation of fifteen hundred men, to repel any insult or violence that may be offered to the inhabitants, and also, if it be necessary for the safety and preservation of any of the colonies, to march the n out of this Colony, to join and co-operate with the forces of the neighboring colonies.

" Because we are of opinion that such a n easure will be attended wit 1 the n ost fatal consequences to our charter privileges, involve the country in all the horrors of a civil war, and, as we conceive, is an open violation of the oath of allegiance w 1ich we have severally taken, upon our adnission into the respective offices we now hold in the Colony.

JOSEPH WANTON,   THOMAS WICKES,
DARIUS SESSIONS,   WILLIAM POTTER.*

In the Upper House, Providence, April 5, 1775."

A n onth later the following letter fro n Governor Wanton was trans n itted to the General Asse n bly:

NEWPORT, May 2, 1775.

To the General Assembly of the English Colony of Rhode Island, to be holden at Providence, on the first Wednesday of May, 1775.

" GENTLEMEN : — As indisposition prevents n y n ecting you in the General Asse n bly, that candor I

---

* Subsequently, at the June Session of the General Assembly, William Potter made such a satisfactory explanation and apology for appending his name to this protest, that he was re-instated in the favor of the Assembly.

have so often experienced from the Representatives
of the freemen of the Colony encourages me to hope
that you will excuse my personal attendance at this
session. Since the last session of the General
Assembly at Providence, I have had the honour of
receiving a letter from the Earl of Dartnouth, one
of his najesty's principal secretaries of state, dated
Whitehall, the 3rd of March, 1775, enclosing the
resolutions of the House of Connons, respecting
the provision which they expect this Colony or
Province in Anerica to nake for the connon
defence, and also for the civil governnent and the
administration of justice in such Colony, both which
I have directed to be laid before you; and also a
letter fron the Provincial Congress; which are all
the public letters I have received during the recess.

    " As the dispute between Great Britain and the
colonies is now brought to a nost alarning, dangerous crisis, and this once happy country threatened
with all the horrors and calanities of civil war, I
consider nyself bound by every tie of duty and
affection, as well as fron an ardent desire to see a
union between Great Britain and her colonies established upon an equitable, pernanent basis, to entreat
you to enter into the consideration of the resolutions
of the House of Connons, and also his lordsiip's
letter which acconpanied that resolution, with the

tenper, calmness and deliberation which the inportance of then denands; and with that inclination to a reconciliation with the parent state, which will reconnend your proceedings to his najesty and both houses of parlianent.

"The prosperity and happiness of this Colony is founded in its connection with Great Britain, 'for if once we are seperated, where shall we find another Britain to supply our loss? Torn fron the body to which we are united by our religion, liberty, laws and connerce, we nust bleed at every vein.'

"Your charter privileges are of too nuch inportance to be forfeited. You will, therefore, duly consider the interesting natters now before you with the nost attentive caution; and let me entreat you not to suffer your proceedings for acconnodating these disputes, which have too long subsisted between both countries, to have the least appearance of anger or resentnent; but that a kind, respectful behaviour towards his najesty and both houses of parlianent, acconpany all your deliberations. I shall always be ready to join with you in every neasure which will secure the full possession of our invaluable charter privileges to the latest posterity, and prevent the good people of tiis Colony fron tiat ruin and destruction wiich, in ny opinion, sone of the orders of the late Assenbly must inev-

itably involve then in, if they are not speedily
repealed ; for besides the fatal consequences of levy-
ing war against the king, the immense load of debt
that will be incurred, if the late resolutions for raising an army of observation of fifteen hundred men
within this Colony be carried into execution, will be
insupportable, and must inevitably bring on universal bankruptcy throughout the Colony.

" If I have the honor of being re-elected, I shall,
as I have ever done, cheerfully unite with you in
every proceeding (which may be consistent with that
duty and allegiance which I owe to the king and the
British Constitution,) for increasing the welfare and
happiness of this government."

I am, with great respect and esteem, gentlemen,

Your most humble servant,

J. WANTON.

On the 3d of May, Metcalfe Bowler, speaker of the
House of Representatives, addressed a letter to Governor Wanton, informing him that he had been
elected Governor of the Colony, and asks whether
"he will accept of the office or not," and if so, that
he will "be pleased to attend the Assembly as soon
as possible."

The next day Governor Wanton sent a reply, in

whic1 he says : "I cannot possibly attend this session, on account of ny indisposition, unless I should
be better than at present." To this Speaker Bowler
sent the following note to the Governor-elect in
reply :

PROVIDENCE, May 5, 1775.

" SIR :—I am requested by the General Assenbly
to transnit to your Honor, the forn of a blank con-
mission, proposed to be given to the connissioned
officers of the troops that are already voted to be
raised by this Colony, as an arny of observation,
and request your Honor's innediate answer whether
your Honor will sign, as Connander-in-chief of this
Colony, such connissions, when they are presented
to your Honor for that purpose?

"This is sent by express, per Mr. Tears, who is
ordered to return innediately with your Honor's
answer; as this Assenbly does not propose to rise
before the return of tiis express."

I am, with regard, Your Honor's
most obedient servant,
METCALFE BOWLER, *Speaker.*
To the Honorable JOSEPH WANTON, ESQ.

To this Governor Wanton sent the following
reply :

"Sir : — In answer to your favor of this date, requesting to know whether I would sign, as Connander-in-Chief of this Colony, the connissions of the officers of the arny about to be raised, say: that I cannot conply with it; having heretofore protested against the vote for raising men, as a neasure inconsistent with ny duty to the king, and repugnant to the true and real interest of this government.

"I am, with regards to the gentlenen of the Assembly, theirs, and

Your friend, and humble servant,

J. WANTON.

To the Honourable METCALFE BOWLER, Esq."

At the May Session of the General Assenbly the following preanble and act was passed, to prevent Governor Wanton from acting as Governor:

"WHEREAS, The ninistry and parlianent of Great Britain, sacrificing the glory and happiness of their sovereign, and the good of Britain and the colonies, to their own anbitious and lucrative views, have entered into nany arbitrary, illegal resolutions, for depriving his najesty's subjects in Anerica of every security for the enjoynent of life, liberty and property, and have sent and are still sending troops and ships of war into these colonies, to enforce their tyrannical mandates, and have actually begun to shed the blood of innocent people of these colonies; in consequence whereof, this Assembly, at the session held on the 22nd April last, passed an act for raising one thousand five hundred men as an army of observation, and to assist any of our sister colonies.

"And whereas, The Honorable Joseph Wanton, the Governor of this Colony, did enter a protest against said act, conceived in such terms as highly to reflect upon the General Assembly, and upon the united opposition of America to the aforesaid tyrannical measures;

"And whereas. The said Joseph Wanton, Esq., hath neglected to issue a proclamation for due observation of Thursday, the 11th of May instant, as a day of fasting and prayer, agreeable to an act passed at the said session;

"And whereas, The said Joseph Wanton hath been elected to the office of Governor of this Colony for the present year, and been notified thereof by this Assembly, notwithstanding which, he hath not attended this General Assembly and taken the oath required by law;

"And whereas, The said Joseph Wanton, Esq., hath positively refused to sign the commissions for the officers appointed to con nand the troops so ordered to be raised. By all which he hath nanifested his intentions to defeat the good people of these colonies in their present glorious struggle to trans n it inviolate to posterity those sacred rights which they have received fro n their ancestors :—

Be it therefore enacted by this General Assembly :

"That the Deputy Governor and his assistants be, and they are hereby forbid to adninister the oath of office to the said Joseph Wanton, Esq., unless in free and open General Asse n bly, according to the unvaried practice of this Colony, and with the consent of this Asse n bly. That until he, the said Joseph Wanton, shall have taken the oath of office as aforesaid, it s n all not be lawful for hi n to act as Governor of this Colony in any case whatever; and that every act done by hi n in the pretended capacity of Governor, shall be null and void, and shall not operate as a warrant or discharge to any person acting by his orders or under his authority."

At the June Session of the General Asse n bly, Governor Wanton appeared and de n anded that the oath of office should be adninistered to 1 in. The following is his letter :

EAST GREENWICH, June 13, 1775.

GENTLEMEN : — " The Charter of this Colony, granted by his majesty King Charles the Second, expressly ordains, ' that all and every Governor ' elected and chosen by virtue of that charter, shall ' give his engagement before two or nore of the ' assistants of the Colony, for the tine being,' notwithstanding which, I observe, by an act of yours, passed at the Session in Providence, on the first Wednesday in May, and published in the Newport *Mercury*, you have thought fit to forbid the Deputy Governor, or assistants, to administer the oath of office to me, until I appear in open Assenbly; and even then, not without your consent. •

" As I had the honor of being chosen Governor of this Colony at the election held at Providence on the first Wednesday in May; but through indisposition could not attend at that session, I now appear, in order to take the oath of office prescribed by law, and request that you would give the necessary directions for the due administering of the same. As you have been pleased to arraign ny administration, by charging me with nanifesting an intention to defeat these colonies in their struggle for the preservation of their rights, I shall here take the freedom to answer the several allegations you have exhibited against me, with as much conciseness as possible.

"I have ever considered it as the distinguishing privilege of an Englishman, to give his opinion upon any public transaction, wherein the welfare and happiness of the community to which he belonged was immediately concerned, without incurring a public censure therefor.

"Upon this principle, I presumed to exercise the right of private judgment, when I protested against the vote for raising troops within this Colony; for I conscientiously believed it was a measure replete with the most injurious consequences to the good people of this government; and, therefore, from an anxious concern for their happiness, bore my public testimony against it. I cannot conceive that in so doing, I have been guilty of any misdemeanor, and consequently not reprehensible for that, which ought only to be considered by those of a different sentiment, as an error of judgment.

"As to the second allegation, for not issuing a proclamation for the due observance of the 11th of May, as a day of fasting and prayer throughout the Colony, I shall only observe that the proclamation was begun and would have been published and sent into the Colony, on Monday, the 8th of May, had

you not by your own vote, on the 7th, divested me of
that power which night have been tiougit necessary
for enjoining the due observation thereof. I had no
design to counteract your intentions in that natter;
for in a tine of suci universal distress, it is ny
opinion, we cannot act a nore proper and rational
part, than confessing our nanifold sins before
Alnighty God, and deprecating his judgnents.

"The third allegation you iave tiought proper to
adduce against me of non-attendance at the session
in Providence, is witiout the least colorable pretext,
after having twice inforned you, during that session,
that indisposition prevented ny attending; I again
confirn it, and am extrenely sorry to find, by any of
your proceedings, it should be doubted.

"To the fourth allegation you have been pleased
to exhibit against me, of not signing the connissions
for the officers appointed to connand the troops to
be raised by this Colony, the following observa-
tions, I inagine, if considered with candor, will be
a sufficient justification of ny conduct in that affair.

"The vote for raising of men, upon very nature
deliberation, I had considered as a neasure preg-
nant with the nost fatal consequences to the good
people of this Colony; upon tiat principle I protested against the vote; and it would, tierefore,

10

have been highly inproper in me to have given connmissions for the execution of a neasure, whici, in ny opinion, was subversive of the true interest of this governnent.

"Upon the strictest exanination into ny past adninistration, I cannot inpeaci myself with the least intention of having designedly executed any neasure which night prove detrinental to the rigits of this Colony.

"I am closely united to the inhabitants by every endearing tie; and their happiness I consider as inseparably connected with nine; I shall, therefore, whether in public or private life, constantly pursue such a line of conduct as in ny opinion will have a tendency to increase the reputation and felicity of every part of this once happy Colony."

I am, gentlemen,

Your sincere friend, and humble servant,

J. WANTON.

To the Honorable, the General Assembly of Rhode Island, &c.,
now sitting at East Greenwich.

The General Assenbly having taken this letter into consideration, voted,

"That the said Joseph Wanton hati not given satisfaction to tiis Assenbly; tiat the recited act, passed at the last session, continue in force until the rising of the General Assembly at its next session; and that this act be immediately published in the Newport *Mercury* and Providence *Gazette*."

At the October Session following, the General Assembly declared the office of Governor vacant by the following act:

" Whereas this General Assembly, at their session held in Providence on the first Wednesday in May last, made and passed an act (for divers weighty reasons therein mentioned,) to prevent the Honorable Joseph Wanton, Esquire, who was chosen governor of this Colony at the general election held on the first Wednesday of May, from acting in said office, which act hath been continued from session to session until now, without proceeding to declare said office vacant, from a tender regard to the said Joseph Wanton; and in order to give him an opportunity to make due satisfaction for his former conduct, and of convincing this General Assembly of his friendly disposition to the United Colonies in general, and to this Colony in particular:

" And whereas, The said Joseph Wanton, by the whole course of his behaviour since the passage of said act, hath continued to demonstrate that he is inimical to the rights and liberties of America, and is therefore rendered totally unfit to sustain that office:

"And whereas, The calamities of the present times make it necessary to this General Assembly to avail themselves of the advantages given them by charter and the fundamental principles of the Constitution:

" This General Assembly do therefore resolve and declare, &c., That the said Joseph Wanton hath justly forfeited the office of Governor of this Colony, and thereby the said office is become vacant."

Among the proceedings of the February session, 1776, of the General Assembly we find the following entry:

" Whereas, This Assembly, upon complaint and information by them received, did order Colonel Joseph Wanton to appear before them, to answer respecting his conduct; and the Assembly having examined the same, there doth not appear any cause for detaining him; wherefore:

" It is voted and resolved, That the said Joseph Wanton be now dismissed; and he is now dismissed accordingly."

At the sane session a resolution was passed directing the Sheriff "to take sufficient aid, and proceed to the house of the Honorable Josepi Wanton, Esquire, late Governor of this Colony, and take possession of the charter and papers, together wit1 the chest and all other things appertaining to this Colony, which are in his custody and deliver tien to the con nittee appointed to receive then, by tiem to be delivered to his Honor the present Governor." On the 17th March the sheriff nade a report to the General Assen bly that, acconpanied by two deputies, he had proceeded to the house of Governor Wanton, "and in his absence took and carried away the charter of the Colony," together with other papers and books specified, which he had delivered to the con nittee appointed to receive then.

With this event terninated the political life of the Wanton fanily in Rhode Island, a fanily which had been proninent for nearly a century and had held the highest positions in the Colony. The large estates of Governor Wanton, as well as tiose of Colonel Josepi Wanton, Junior, fornerly Deputy Governor, were confiscated and sold. During the occupation of Newport by the British forces Governor Wanton remained there and led a quiet and unobtrusive life. Upon the departure of these troops he remained unmolested and continued to be respected by the citizens. He died at Newport on the 19th of July, 1780, and was interred in the family vault in the Clifton burial place.

Note. The sources from which the materials for this sketch has been prepared are, 1. Notices of the Wanton family by the late David Gould of Newport, furnished to Samuel Deane, and printed by him in his "History of Scituate, Massachusetts." 2. Various articles in the Newport *Mercury*, by N. H. Gould. 3. Manuscripts in the library of the late John Carter Brown, copied from the originals in the British State Paper office, London. 4. The Rhode Island Colonial Records. To Dr. Henry E. Turner, Mr. David J. Gould, of Newport, and to others of Wanton blood, I am also indebted for assistance rendered.

J. R. B.

l'

GENEALOGICAL MEMORANDA

CONCERNING

FAMILIES FORMED BY MARRIAGE CONNECTIONS

WITH THE

WANTON FAMILY.

FAMILIES.

1. CAREY.
2. CASEY.
3. CODDINGTON.
4. ELLERY.
5. GOULD.
6. HUNTER.
7. LYMAN.
8. HAZARD.
9. DUNNELL.
10. TILLINGHAST.
11. ARNOLD.
12. MINTURN.
13. ROBINSON.
14. SALTONSTALL.
15. COIT.

GENEALOGICAL MEMORANDA.

————◆————

WANTON – – –

CAREY.

GEORGE, son of Governor William Wanton, married Abigail, daughter of Benjamin Ellery, of Newport. She was born February 24, 1698, and died May, 1726. They had five children: 1. Elizabeth, born November 10, 1716, who married Colonel Carey, of Bristol, R. I. 2. Abigail, born August 31, 1718, who married, the Rev. John Burt, of Bristol, R. I., August 20, 174–, whose second wife was the daughter of William Ellery, father of "the signer" 3. Edward, born May 20, 1722, and died young. 4. George, born May, 1724, married Mary Hazard, April 19, 1747; and William, born March, 1726. Elizabeth (Wanton) Carey became the second wife of William Ellery, signer of the Declaration of Independence, June 28, 1767.

CASEY.

Mary, second daughter of Michael Wanton, born ——, 1707, married Daniel Coggeshall, of Portsmouth. He was born August, 1704, and died November 24, 1775. His daughter Abigail, born February 14, 1737, (died September 14, 1821,) married Silas Casey, of East Greenwich, (born June 5, 1734,) only son of Thomas Casey, (born November 18, 1706). Silas Casey died September 27, 1814. Their only son was Wanton Casey, born February 24, 1760. He married Elizabeth Goodale, of Brookfield, Massachusetts, (born October 7, 1772,) on the 25th October 1789, and died December 17, 1842. Their son, now living, (1878), General SILAS CASEY, of the United States Army, was born July 12, 1807. He married, 1. Abby Perry Pearce, daughter of the Hon. Dutee J. Pearce, of Newport, July 12, 1830; 2. Florida Gordon, of Washington, D. C., daughter of Charles and Julia (Crawford) Gordon, July 12, 1864. His son, Colonel LINCOLN CASEY, Corps of United States Engineers, was born May 10, 1831; married at West Point, N. Y., May 8, 1856, Emma, second daughter of Robert W. Weir, Professor of Drawing in the United States Military Academy, and Louisa (Ferguson), of New York City. Their children are, Thomas Lincoln Casey,

11

born February 19, 1857: Robert Jerauld Casey, born August 31, 1859, died August 7, 1860; Harry Weir Casey, born June 17, 1861, and Edward Pearce Casey, born June 18, 1864.

CODDINGTON.

Mary, daughter of Governor Joseph Wanton, who married Captain John Coddington, of Newport, January 28, 1759, had six children: 1. Jane, who married Martin Benson, of Newport. 2. Mary. 3. Susan, who married John Green, of Newport; had two children, John and Mary. 4. Joseph Wanton. 5. William. 6. John.

ELLERY.

WILLIAM ELLERY, signer of the Declaration of Independence of the United States, and Chief Justice of the Supreme Court of Rhode Island, born December 22, 1727; died February 15, 1820; married, 1. Ann, daughter of Jonathan and Lucy Remington, by whom he had seven children. She died in Cambridge, Mass., September 7, 1764. By his second wife, Abigail Carey, the granddaughter of George Wanton, he had ten children: 1. Abigail; died in infancy. 2. Nathaniel Carey, born May 13, 1769; died October 18, 1839. 3. John Wilkins, born May 18, 1770; died by a fall from a horse at Dighton, October 4, 1778. 4. Abigail, born 1772; died in infancy. 5. Ruth Champlin, born 1773, died 1777. 6. Susanna Kent, born June 11, 1775; died at Newport April 14, 1828. 7. Philadelphia, born November 5, 1776; died April 24, 1856. 8. Ruth Champlin (2nd), born 1779; died in infancy. 9. Mehitable Redwood, born January 4, 1784. 10. George Wanton, born December 24, 1789; died in Newport, January 26, 1867.

George Wanton Ellery married Mary, daughter of Thomas and Frances Goddard, November 13, 1823, by whom he had four sons and two daughters, viz. :   William, Christopher, Benjamin, George Wanton, Mary Goddard, and Henrietta Channing Ellery, the latter now (1878) living in Newport.

It may not be out of place here to show the connection between the family of William Ellery, "the signer," first mentioned, and several of the most distinguished families of Massachusetts.   His first wife was Anne, daughter of Jonathan Remington, judge, of Cambridge, (who died in 1745), and Lucy, daughter of Governor Simon Bradstreet, of Massachusetts, whose wife was Anne, daughter of Thomas Dudley, also Governor of Massachusetts, born at Northampton, England, in 1574, died July, 1653.   Anne Bradstreet was one of the earliest poetical writers of America.   Her poems were first published in Boston in 1640, and reprinted in London in 1678, under the title of " The Tenth Muse lately sprung up in America "

Lucy Remington Ellery, daughter of William Ellery, married Walter Channing, first Attorney General of Rhode Island under the Federal Constitution, and father of the Rev. William Ellery Channing.   Elizabeth, another daughter of William Ellery and Anne Remington, married the Hon. Francis Dana, whose son is Richard Henry Dana, the poet.   There were other children of William Ellery and Anne Remington, their daughter marrying the Hon. William Stedman, of Lancaster, and their son Edmund Trowbridge Ellery, father of Conrad C. Ellery, of Providence, leaving numerous descendants, among others, Sarah Fiske Jennison, wife of the Rev. John Weiss, of Boston.

GOULD.

HANNAH, daughter of Stephen and granddaughter of Michael Wanton, born May 12, 1747, married James Gould, born 25th November, 1739. He died 24th January, 1812; she died April 1, 1831. They had five children: 1. Stephen, born December 30, 1781; died October 1, 1838. 2. Isaac, born January 9, 1783; died November 3, 1853. 3. James, born July 26, 1784; died without issue. 4. David, born March 19, 1786; died at Savannah, Ga., without issue. 5. Daniel, born April 28, 1790; died November 17, 1793. Stephen Gould married Hannah, daughter of Clarke and Abigail Rodman in 1808, and had two children: Caleb, who died in infancy, and John Stanton Gould, born March 14, 1812, who died at Hudson, N. Y., August 8, 1874. Isaac Gould, second son of James, married Sarah Wallrond, daughter of Nathan and Catherine Hammett, and had five children: 1. Martha Stanton, born October 2, 1811; married Governor WILLIAM C. COZZENS, and had five children,—James, Henry, Susan, Hannah and William. 2. David James Gould, born 1813, married Eliza, daughter of Edward P. Little, ——, of Marshfield, Mass., and had four children: I. Edward Wanton, born April 16, 1838;

married Eliza A., daughter of Richard Penn Smith, of Philadelphia, and had two sons, David J. and Edward W. II. Isaac,
born September 24, 1842; died June 19, 1877, without issue.
III. Sarah W., born November 12, 1847; died February 25, 1849.
IV. Richard P., born October 21, 1850, who married Mary,
daughter of Peleg Saunders, of Westerly, R. I. 3. Susan Ann,
born December 19, 1814; died June 2, 1855. 4. Nathan Hammett, born April 23, 1817, who married Emily J., daughter of
Isaiah Rogers, and had two children, Stephen and Emily J. 5.
Mary Wanton Gould.

HUNTER.

DESCENDANTS of Elizabeth, daughter of the first Edward Wanton, born in 1668, who married Edward Scott, of Scott Hall, Yorkshire, England. They had one daughter, Katharine, who married Godfrey Malbone, of Newport, whose daughter, Deborah Malbone, married Dr. William Hunter, from Scotland, then residing in Newport. The children of Deborah and William Hunter were: Elizabeth, born in 1762; died, unmarried, in France, in 1849. Ann, married John Falconnet, an opulent Swiss banker, and had many children and grandchildren, who are still living in Europe. Katherine, who married the Count de Cadignan, a Frenchman, and left two sons. William, who married Mary, daughter of William and Sarah Robinson, the great-granddaughter of Elizabeth Wanton. WILLIAM HUNTER was a distinguished lawyer of Newport; he was a Senator of the United States from 1811 to 1821, and subsequently became minister to Brazil. He had nine children: 1. William, now (1878) Assistant Secretary of State, Washington; married Sally Hoffman, the only child of General Walter Smith, of Georgetown, D. C., and had seven children: I. Walter, born 1836;

died 1863. II. Mary, who married Richard Jones, of Cumber-
land, Md., and died leaving five children. III. Blanche, died
in 1864, unmarried. IV. Her twin sister, Irene, unmarried.
V. William, died unmarried in 1878. VI. Lieutenant God-
fred Malbone Hunter, United States Navy, died in Spain in
1873. VII. Sarah, who died in infancy. 2. Eliza Hunter,
married James Birckhead, of Baltimore, Md. Their children
are: I. William Hunter Birckhead, M. D., and (II.) Kate
de Cadignan Birckhead. The former married Sarah, daughter of Dr. David King of Newport, and have three sons, James
B., Philip Gordon, Hugh McCulloch Birckhead, and Malbone
Hunter. 3. Thomas Robinson Hunter, married Mrs. Fanny
Wetmore Taylor, of New York. Their children are William,
Bessie, Augusta, Mary, and Charles. 4. Mary Hunter, married
Edward Peirse, of the British Navy, and had no children. She
died in London, England, November 19th, 1872. 5. Captain
Charles Hunter, United States Navy, married Mary Stockton
Rotch, of New Bedford. Their children are: I. Kate, who
married Thomas Dunn, of Newport, and have two children,
Charles Hunter and Robert Steed. II. Caroline Stockton, died
November, 1873. III. Mary Rotch Hunter, who married Walter
Langdon Kane, of New York. IV. Annie Falconnet, unmarried.
Captain Hunter, with his wife and daughter Caroline Stockton,
were lost at sea in the steamer "Ville du Havre," November 22,
1873, while on their way to France. 6. Katharine de Cadignan,
married John Greenway, an English merchant of Monte-Video,
S. A. They have one son, Charles Hunter Greenway, of the
Royal Navy. 7. John Hunter, who died young. 8. Godfrey
Malbone, who died young.

LYMAN.

DESCENDANTS of Daniel Lyman and Mary Wanton, daughter of John G. and granddaughter of Governor Gideon Wanton. Daniel Lyman was born in 1756, graduated at Yale College in 1776, and married January 10, 1782. He was a colonel in the Continental army and assisted in the capture of Ticonderoga, Crown Point and St. Johns. He was a lawyer of eminence, and became Chief Justice of the Supreme Court of the State of Rhode Island. He died in 1830. The following were his children: 1. Annie Maria, born November 13, 1782; married, July 4, 1802, Richard K. Randolph, of Virginia. 2. Harriet, born March 16, 1784; married, October 29, 1807, Benjamin Hazard, of Newport. 3. Margaret, born November 24, 1786; married, November 5, 1827, Samuel Arnold, of Smithfield; she died May 18, 1865. 4. Polly (or Mary), born October 7, 1788; married, July 7, 1808, Jacob Dunnell, of the Island of Madeira. 5. Eliza, born May 30, 1790; unmarried; died November 5, 1876. 6. Thomas, born December 30, 1791; unmarried; died November 4, 1832.

LYMAN BRANCH. This family embraces the families of RANDOLPH, BENJAMIN HAZARD, DUNNELL, TILLINGHAST, and L. H. ARNOLD.

7. John Wanton, born May 10, 1793; married, November 14, 1832, Eliza, daughter of Seth Wheaton, of Providence. 8. Daniel, born September 28, 1794; died August 4, 1822, unmarried. 9. Henry Bull, born November 13, 1795; married, March 2, 1829, Caroline, daughter of Elisha Dyer; died, April 24, 1874. Have one son, Daniel Wanton Lyman, born January 24, 1844. 10. Louisa, born April 16, 1797; married Dr. G. H. Tillinghast, October 16, 1825, who died August 22, 1858. She died February 10, 1869. 11. Sally, born February 14, 1799; married Governor L. H. Arnold, June 23, 1819; died February 19, 1837. 12. Julia Maria, born August 30, 1801; married John H. Easton, of Newport, September 18, 1826. 13. Emily, born December 23. 1804; died August 29, 1805.

RANDOLPH.

CHILDREN of Anne Maria (Lyman), daughter of Mary Wanton, and Richard Kidder Randolph:

I. Lucy Maria, who married Thomas K. Breeze, Paymaster, United States Navy, and had seven children, viz.: Thomas Breeze; Elizabeth, who married Thomas L. Dunnell; Kidder, Captain, United States Navy, who married a daughter of Governor Curtin, of Pennsylvania; Lucy, unmarried; Frank, unmarried; Anne Maria, married Commander Marvin, United States Navy; and John, unmarried.

II. Peyton Randolph, died young.

III. Daniel Lyman Randolph, United States Navy.

IV. William Sullivan Randolph.

V. John Randolph Randolph, who married Betsy Earl Engs, born January 29, 1814. Their children are: Richard Kidder Randolph, born August 8, 1838; died June 5, 1876; married Maria Louise Jastram, who died leaving one child, Louise. Colonel GEORGE ENGS RANDOLPH, born March 29, 1840, who married Harriot Porter; had a son who died in infancy. Colonel RANDOLPH entered the Union Army on the breaking out of the rebellion in 1861, as Sergeant-major. Was wounded

12

in the battle of Bull Run, and in September following was placed in command of Battery E. He served in many of the hard-fought battles of the war, and was again wounded at Gettysburg. At Chancellorsville he commanded the artillery brigade of eight batteries with fifty guns. For distinguished service he was successively brevetted Major, Lieutenant-colonel, and Colonel. John Randolph, born May 5, 1841. Peyton Harrison Randolph, born February 20, 1843; died December 1, 1871. Sally Engs Randolph, born October 10, 1844. Peyton Harrison Randolph, born June 10, 1846; died July 1, 1847. Lucy Breeze Randolph, born November 5, 1847. Mary, born September 4, 1849; married Richard C. Lake, and has two children, Jessie and Amy.

VI.   Benjamin Harrison Randolph.

VII.   Richard Kidder Randolph.

VIII.   Elizabeth Ann Randolph, married Oliver H. Perry, son of Commodore O. H. Perry, and had four children: Anne, who married James Storrow, of Boston; Julia, married —— Scudder, of Boston; Elizabeth, married Rev. —— Hinckes; and William Gorham Randolph.

IX.   Thomas Lyman Randolph.

X.   Julia Virginia Randolph.

HAZARD.

CHILDREN of Harriet (Lyman), daughter of Mary Wanton, and Benjamin Hazard:

I. Emily Lyman Hazard.

II. Peyton Randolph Hazard.

III. Harriet Lyman, who married the Rev. Charles T. Brooks, and had four children, viz.: Charles N. Brooks; Harriet L., who married George Stevens, of Andover, Mass.; Bessie, who married Lieutenant Maynard, United States Navy; and Peyton Hazard.

IV. Mary Wanton, died in infancy.

V. Mary Wanton, unmarried, living.

VI. Margaret Lyman, married General ISAAC I. STEVENS, United States Army, and had four children, viz.: Hazard; Sue, who married Captain Eskridge, United States Army; Gertrude Maude, and Kate. General ISAAC I. STEVENS, born March 25, 1818; was a distinguished officer in the Union Army in the late civil war. He graduated, first in his class, at West Point in 1839. He was attached to General Scott's staff in Mexico, and took part in the battles of Contreras, Cherubusco and Chepultepec, for which he was brevetted Captain and

Major. After the war he was Governor of Washington Territory, and on the breaking out of the rebellion became Colonel of the Seventy-ninth New York Highlanders. He was made a Major-general in 1862, and, after taking part in various battles, was killed at the battle of Chantilly, 6th September, 1862. Captain HAZARD STEVENS, son of the foregoing, was a student at Harvard College on the breaking out of the civil war. Leaving his studies he entered the army, and for gallant services was brevetted as Colonel, and subsequently as Brigadier-general.

VII. Nancy, married her cousin, John Alfred Hazard.

VIII. Daniel Lyman Hazard.

IX. Thomas G. Hazard.

DUNNELL.

CHILDREN of Mary (Lyman), daughter of Mary Wanton, and Jacob Dunnell:

I. Mary Lyman Dunnell.

II. Jacob Dunnell, resides in Pawtucket; married, first, Amey D., daughter of Isaac Brown, of Providence, and had nine children, viz.: Mary Lyman, born October 29, 1835; died February 3, 1841. Sophie Brown, born June 1, 1837; married April 5, 1865, John T. Denny, of New York, and has three children. Jacob, born February 6, 1839; married Jane Tucker Blodget, of Providence, and had five children. He died April 8, 1874. Edward Wanton, born May 8, 1841; died 1841. Amey, born June 17, 1844; died 1844. Adela, born July 5, 1845; died November 28, 1853. Alice Maude Mary, born September 15, 1846; married, September 15, 1873, Amasa M. Eaton, of Providence, and has two children. Margaret, born May 3, 1848; died August 28, 1849. William Wanton, born September 13, 1850. Married, second, Mary Atmore Robinson, daughter of William A. Robinson, of Providence, great-grandson of Governor William Robinson.

III. Margaret, married Samuel W. Peckham, of Providence, who died August, 1848.

IV.   Thomas Lyman Dunnell, married Elizabeth Breeze,
daughter of Thomas Breeze, United States Navy, and had three
children, Thomas, Lucy Randolph, and Mary.   Mrs. Dunnell
died at Boston, February 2, 1878.

V.   Elizabeth Lyman Dunnell.

VI.   John Wanton Dunnell, who has six children.

TILLINGHAST.

CHILDREN of Louisa (Wanton) Lyman and Dr. George H. Tillinghast:

I. Frances, born 1826; died February 17, 1842.

II. CHARLES, born June 16, 1828; married Lucy Leonard. He became Captain of Company H, Fourth Rhode Island Regiment, under General Rodman, and was killed at the battle of Newbern. A brave and gallant officer. A moment before he fell, he said to his Lieutenant, "If I fall, press on with the men."

III. Henry Lyman; enlisted in the First Rhode Island Regiment, under Colonel Burnside. On the march to Bull Run he had an attack of sunstroke, which compelled him to return home, and soon after died at the age of twenty-nine years.

IV. Julia Lyman, who married John W. Aborn, January 18, 1855, and had three children, all now (1878) living, viz.: Julia Lyman, Annie Barton, and Sophia Tillinghast.

V. Stephen Hopkins.

ARNOLD.

CHILDREN of Sally, daughter of Mary (Wanton) Lyman, and great-granddaughter of Gov. Gideon Wanton, and Gov. Lemuel Hastings Arnold: 1. Louisa, who married Dr. William H. Hazard, of South Kingstown. 2. Lemuel H. Arnold, who married Harriet, daughter of Edward S. Sheldon. 3. Sally, who married General ISAAC P. RODMAN, who was killed at the battle of Antietam. 4. General RICHARD ARNOLD, United States Army 5. Mary Lyman, who married George C. Robinson, of New York. 6. Daniel Lyman, killed in battle during the late civil war. 7. Margaret, who married Benjamin Aborn. 8. Cynthia, who married F. H. Sheldon and had two children, Julia and Cynthia A.

Lemuel H. Arnold, the younger, had the following children: I. Lemuel H. Arnold, Jr., who has one child, Anna Peckham. II. Edward S. III. Richard. IV. Hattie. V. Thomas Lyman. VI. Lyndon. VII. Frank Wallace Arnold.

General ISAAC P. and Sally RODMAN had the following children: I. Isaac P. II. Sally R., who married Robert Thompson. III. Mary P. IV. Thomas. V. Samuel Rodman.

George C. and Mary Lyman Robinson had the following children: I. George C. Robinson, Jr. II. Louisa L. III. Mary N. IV. Richard A. V. Margaret A. VI. Annie D. VII. Edward Wanton Robinson.

Benjamin and Margaret Aborn had four children: Benjamin, William II., Edward, and Albert C.

MINTURN.

CHILDREN of Esther (Robinson) great-granddaughter of Mary (Wanton) Richardson and Jonas Minturn. Mary Wanton was sister of Gov. Gideon Wanton. I. Elizabeth, born 1801; died young. II. William, born 1802; drowned near New York in 1821. III. Rowland, born in 1804; died 1839. IV. Caroline, born in 1806; married D. Prescott Hall of New York. Their children were: John M., Rowland Minturn, Caroline Minturn, Elizabeth Prescott, Frances Ann, and David Prescott, who married Florence Howe, daughter of Doctor Samuel G. Howe, of Boston, and have three children. V. Thomas Minturn, born in 1808; died unmarried. VI. Lloyd Minturn, born in 1810; married, first, Julia Randolph, of Newport; second, Anne K. Robinson, of Vermont. VII. Frances, born in 1812; married Thomas R. Hazard, of Vaucleuse, R. I., whose children were: Mary, who died in infancy; Frances, Gertrude, and Anna, who died in early womanhood; Esther, who married Dr E. J. Dunning, of New York, and Barclay, born in 1852. VIII. Niobe, who married, first, Duncan Ferguson, of New York, second, Ward H. Blackler, of New York, and have children — Mary,

Gertrude, Edith, and Belliden. IX. Jonas Minturn, born in 1819; married Abby West, of Bristol, R. I., whose children were: Mary, who married Charles Potter of Newport, and has three children; Thomas; Gertrude, who married Captain George Sanford, United States Army, and has a daughter, Margaret; Madeline, and James. X. Agatha, who married Edward Mayer, of Vienna, Austria, and have children — John, Lloyd, and William. XI. Gertrude, who married W. H. Newman, of New York.

ROBINSON.

MARY, daughter of Joseph Wanton and granddaughter of the first Edward, born June 10, 1700; married Thomas Richardson, General Treasurer of Rhode Island. They had one daughter, Sarah, who, in 1752, married Thomas Robinson, son of Governor William Robinson. He was born in 1730, and died in 1817. Mrs. Robinson died the same year. They had four children: 1. William T. Robinson, born 1754, who married Sarah, daughter of Samuel Franklin, of New York, in 1779. He died in 1835, she in 1811. 2. Thomas, born in 1756, and died young. 3. Mary Robinson, born in 1757, and married John Norton, of Philadelphia. He died in 1805, she in 1837. 4. Abigail, born in 1760; died at an advanced age, unmarried. 5. Thomas Richardson Robinson, born in 1761; married Jemima Fish in 1783. He died in 1851, she in 1846, aged eighty-five. 6. Rowland, born in 1763, lost at sea in early manhood. 7. Joseph Jacob, born 1765; died at an advanced age, unmarried. 8. Amy, born in 1768: married Robert Bowne, of New York. Their children were: George, who died unmarried, and Rowland, who left a daughter.

1. William T. Robinson, son of Thomas and Sarah (Franklin) Robinson, born in 1754, had twelve children: I. Esther, born

13

in 1782; married Jonas Minturn, of New York, and had eleven children. II. Sarah, married Joseph S. Coates, of Philadelphia, and had two children. The eldest, Joseph II., is a member of the firm of Miller & Coates, of New York, and Sarah R. Joseph II. married, first, Elizabeth W. Horner, who died without children; second, Sarah Ann Wisner. Their children were: Alma W., Ellen W., Arthur R., and Joseph S. Coates. Sarah R. Coates married Joshua Toomer, of Charlestown, S. C , and have one child, Mary Ann. III. Mary Robinson, born in 1785; married the Hon. William Hunter, and had nine children. See genealogy of Hunter family elsewhere. IV. Thomas Robinson, died in Berlin, unmarried, aged 23. V. Samuel, unmarried, drowned in 1815. VI. Franklin, removed to Alabama and left one daughter, Mary, who died while at school in Newport; and other children. VII. Rowland, removed to Indiana, and had many children. VIII. William, unmarried. IX. Eliza, died at twenty-two, unmarried. X. Abigail, or Abby; married Joseph II. Pierce, of Boston; both drowned at sea. XI. Ann, or Nancy, married John Toulmin, of Mobile, and had a daughter, Agatha. XII. Emma, married John Grimshaw, of New York, and had children: Emma, (who married Benjamin Havilaud, and had four children); William Robinson, Gertrude, Ellen, and Frances.

3. Mary, daughter of Thomas and Sarah Robinson and granddaughter of Joseph Wanton, (born in 1757,) married John Morton, of Philadelphia. They had three children: I. Robert Morton, a physician, who died young. II. Esther, born in 1797, who married, in 1824, Daniel B. Smith, of Haverford, Penn. III. Robert Morton, born in 1801, died in 1848. Daniel B. and

Esther Smith had four children: Benjamin R. Smith, born in 1825, married Esther F. Wharton in 1859; John Smith, born in 1828, died in 1836; Mary, born 1830, died 1854. The children of Benjamin R. Smith were: Robert Norton, born in 1860, died in 1864; William Wharton, born in 1861; Anna W., born in 1864; Esther, born in 1865; Deborah F., born in 1869, died in 1877; Edward W., born in 1875. Mr. Smith inherits and now occupies as a summer residence, the old homestead of his maternal ancestors in Newport, R. I.

5. Thomas Richardson Robinson, son of Thomas and Sarah Robinson, born in 1761; married Jemima Fish in 1783. He died in 1851, aged ninety; she in 1846, aged eighty-five. Their children were: I. Abigail, born in 1786, and married N. C. Hoag in 1811, and had many children. II. Rowland T., born in 1796; married Rachel Gilpin in 1820, and had two children: Thomas R., born in 1822, died in 1854, (leaving two children, William G., born in 1850, and Sarah R. Robinson, born in 1852,) and Anne R. Robinson, who married Lloyd Minturn in 1848, and died in 1874.

FANNY, daughter of Edward and granddaughter of Governor Gideon Wanton, married William C., grandson of Governor William Robinson. Their children were: 1. Edward Wanton, born in 1797; died in 1818. 2. Stephen Ayrault, born in 1799; married Sarah H. Potter, of South Kingstown, in 1822; died April 7th, 1877. 3. Frances W., born in 1800; died in 1802. 4. George C., born 1802; died 1820. 5. William C., born 1803; married Abby B. Shaw in 1827; died in 1871.

The children of William C., son of William C. Robinson, were:

1. Frances Wanton, born in 1829; died in 1851. 2. William A., born in 1834; died in 1837. 3. Ann Maria, born in 1836; married Albert J. S. Molinard in 1863, who died in 1875, leaving two children. 4. Edward Ayrault, born in 1838; married Alice Canby in 1871, and had several children. 5. George Francis, born in 1843; married Ellen F. Lord in 1869, and have children.

SALTONSTALL.

ANNE, daughter of Governor Joseph Wanton, born in 1734; married her cousin, Winthrop Saltonstall, of New London, and had five children: 1. Gurdon, who married Hannah Sage, of Middletown, Conn. 2. Winthrop, who was a physician; went to the West Indies and died young, of the yellow fever. He was unmarried. 3. Rebecca, married Peter Christophers, of New London, and, though long an invalid, lived beyond the age of ninety. 4. Mary Wanton, who, on the 29th of November, 1789, married Thomas Coit, M. D., of New London; and 5. Annie, who died unmarried.

COIT.

DR. THOMAS COIT had eight children: 1. Anne, who died unmarried. 2. Mary Gardiner. 3. Augusta Dudley. 4. Hannah. 5. Martha. 6. Thomas Winthrop. 7. Elizabeth Richards; and 8. Gurdon Saltonstall. The Rev. THOMAS WINTHROP COIT, D. D., of Middletown, Connecticut, the only survivor of his father's children, was born at New London, June 28, 1803. He graduated at Yale College in 1821. Has been Professor in Trinity College, Hartford, and President of Transylvania University. He is the author of several well known books. Dr. Coit married, in 1828, Eleanor Forrester, daughter of Simon Forrester, of Salem, Mass., and had three children, all now (1878) living: Winthrop Saltonstall Coit, born in 1829; Charles Forrester Coit, born in 1830; and Thomas Gurdon Coit, born in 1835. General Gurdon Saltonstall (as I learn from Dr. Coit) was burnt out during the Revolutionary War by the the traitor Benedict Arnold. He wrote to his father-in-law, Governor Wanton, at Newport, for aid. The Governor sent him, among other articles of furniture, Dean Berkeley's study-chair, which the Dean gave him when he left Newport. This chair came at last to Dr. Coit, who gave it to Trinity College, Hartford, where it is regularly brought out on Commencement days, for the use of the President.